VOICE PRINT

VOICE PRINT

How to Leave a Lasting Impression Every Time You Speak

SALLY PROSSER

PRAISE FOR *VOICEPRINT*

"In this world we need a voice more than ever, and *Voiceprint* gives us the tools to speak with clarity, heart and humour. A must-read for anyone who wants to communicate well, which in reality is any human being!"
Dr Sonia Henry, Best-selling author and medical practitioner

"As a TV presenter, my voice is an essential tool to bring stories to life. In *Voiceprint*, Sally has been able to reveal how anyone can harness this tool for genuine connection and meaningful change. Honest, practical and refreshingly bold."
Katrina Blowers, Seven News Presenter and Journalist

"Invaluable for speakers, would-be speakers and anyone who wants to have their voice heard."
Adjunct Professor Sophie Scott OAM, university of Sydney

"Proper laugh-out-loud funny. The way Sally wraps her lessons inside stories is why this gem isn't just another 'how-to' book destined to collect dust on your shelf. If you've ever doubted the power of your voice, this book will become your bible."
Nicole Joy, founder She Speaks Academy

"*Voiceprint* is a bold, brilliant anthem for reclaiming your power through your voice. Equal parts science, soul, and sass, this is the modern manifesto we didn't know we needed."
Prof. Catherine Ball, Scientific Futurist

"The most holistic book on voice I have come across, written with humour and credibility, this is a must-read for anyone who has struggled to be heard."
Simone Heng, Award-winning author and speaker

First published in 2025 by Dean Publishing
PO Box 119
Mt. Macedon, Victoria, 3441
Australia
deanpublishing.com

Copyright © Sally Prosser

All rights reserved. No part of this publication may be reproduced, stored in a retrieval system or transmitted in any way or by any means, electronic, mechanical, photocopying, recording or otherwise, without the prior written permission of the author and publisher.

Cataloguing-in-Publication Data
National Library of Australia
Title: Voiceprint
ISBN: 978-0-64893-861-3
Category: Self-Help/Communication & Voice

The views and opinions expressed in this book are those of the author and do not necessarily reflect the official policy or position of any other agency, publisher, organisation, employer, or company. Assumptions made in the analysis are not reflective of the position of any entity other than the author(s) — and, these views are always subject to change, revision, and rethinking at any time.

The author, publisher or organisations are not to be held responsible for misuse, reuse, recycled and cited and/or uncited copies of content within this book by others.

The ideas within this book are inspired from the author's experiences and career practices. The reader is advised to always seek professional advice according to their specific needs whether business, career, health, or medical.

The stories and ideas in this book stem from the author's personal experiences and are created from memory. Many details in this book are based on the author's life experiences and unique worldview, some names and identifying details have been changed to protect the privacy of individuals.

*In loving memory of my
speech and drama teacher and mentor,
Carole Miller, whose voice shaped mine.*

*Thank you for instilling in me the
confidence and skills to speak and be heard.*

CONTENTS

INTRODUCTION 1

PART ONE: IDENTIFY YOUR VOICEPRINT

CHAPTER 1: HANG ON, A WHAT-PRINT? 7

CHAPTER 2: THE VP BLACK MARKET 15

CHAPTER 3: PUT A STAKE IN YOUR SOUND 23

CHAPTER 4: OPERATION VOICE CUPID 37

CHAPTER 5: GO QUIET TO BE HEARD 47

CHAPTER 6: GROUND AND BREATHE 59

PART TWO: IMPRESS WITH YOUR VOICEPRINT

CHAPTER 7: THE V.O.I.C.E FORMULA 79

CHAPTER 8: V = VIBRATIONS 85

CHAPTER 9: O = OPENNESS 105

CHAPTER 10: I = INTONATION 119

CHAPTER 11: C = CLARITY 135

CHAPTER 12: E = EXPRESSION 155

PART THREE: INVEST IN YOUR VOICEPRINT

CHAPTER 13: SPEAK YOUR BLUEPRINT 173

CHAPTER 14: PROLONG YOUR PRINT 189

CHAPTER 15: ACCESS ALL AREAS...201

CHAPTER 16: PRINT IT ON THE RECORD 213

CHAPTER 17: TAKE THE GLOVES OFF............................... 223

VOICEPRINT MANIFESTO... 230

ACKNOWLEDGEMENTS.. 234

BONUSES... 236

ABOUT THE AUTHOR..237

PERMISSIONS 239

ENDNOTES 240

INTRODUCTION

"Read the section I've marked – just do your best."

Mrs Miller handed me a worn copy of *George's Marvellous Medicine* by Roald Dahl. My little 8-year-old heart was pounding. This was a big deal. I had my heart set on speech and drama lessons, and everyone knew Mrs Miller was the best in town. You essentially had to audition to work with her.

When I started reading, her eyes lit up, and a smile spread across her face. I kept going – reading with as much expression as I could muster.

At the end, she said, "Sal, that VOICE!"

I was hooked. Speech and drama became my favourite extracurricular activity, and Mrs Miller became one of the most important mentors in my life. She sparked and nurtured a love of using my voice to express myself – through poetry, prose, characterisations, school speeches

INTRODUCTION

and just sharing what was on my heart.

Over the years, our lessons morphed into part speech training and part therapy sessions – unpacking everything from sibling spats to failed school captain bids, the latest boy trouble, and the agony of why I got an A instead of an A+. My teenage perfectionist vibes were strong.

One of the deepest sadnesses in my life is that Mrs Miller passed away during COVID-19 lockdowns and I never got to say goodbye.

Mrs Miller set me on a life path that allowed me to step into my soul's purpose and mission.

That first day, she handed me the kind of medicine that had nothing to do with George's concoction – it was the magic and medicine of my own voice.

**Now, I want you to experience
the magic of yours.**

Maybe you're here because you want to conquer your fear of public speaking. Maybe you know your voice is the key to advancing your career or growing your business. Perhaps you want to communicate more effectively for everyday life – wrangling renovations,

INTRODUCTION

negotiating big purchases, answering phone calls, or simply upping the quality of your pillow talk.

Whether you've followed my journey for years or you're meeting me for the first time on these pages – welcome! I'm so grateful you're here. I poured my heart, soul and all my best corny jokes into this book, so I truly hope you enjoy the ride. There was no ghostwriter involved – I wrote every word on the page and spoke every word in the audiobook. If I'm asking you to honour and embrace the power of *your* voiceprint, it's only fair you hear all this from mine.

PART ONE

IDENTIFY YOUR VOICEPRINT

"Don't just speak,
leave an imprint
that lasts."

SALLY PROSSER

CHAPTER 1
HANG ON, A WHAT-PRINT?

"That's it, just a bit harder."

The young police constable cradled my 18-year-old thumb, gently rocking it back and forth on the ink pad. This wasn't as erotic as it sounds, but we *were* getting 50 shades of barely visible grey.

"Push as hard as you can." The ink pad was drying up by the minute. People were walking past casting judgey looks.

"I'm not a criminal," I bleated.

I was one of those annoying high-achieving students off on a Rotary Youth Exchange adventure to Brazil and needed a police check for the visa.

"Don't worry, you wouldn't be in this section if you'd

committed a crime," the constable reassured me.

After pressing with so much force the page almost tore, he announced, "Yep, we've got 'em!"

And just like that, my prints officially entered police files – every unique loop, spiral and arch.

Now, 20-ish years on, I still have no criminal record; however, I *do* have something that would be criminal to keep quiet.

Everywhere we go, we leave prints.

Some prints you can see with the naked eye – footprints in the sand, colourful handprint paintings by children, fingerprints in ink, even lip prints on a serviette. Others you need an ultraviolet light or fluorescent powder to see, like in crime shows. Retinal and iris prints are measured with special imaging tools. And some prints, you can't see at all – like the invisible mark you leave on the world every time you speak.

**Spoiler alert – I'm talking about
your VOICEPRINT.**

A strong voiceprint makes people lean in when you

start talking and echoes in their hearts long after you stop. It's heard and *felt*.

By the way, the image of the sound wave on the cover of this book is the visual representation of me saying, "*Voiceprint* by Sally Prosser."

What is a voiceprint?

Your voiceprint is made up of hundreds of distinct factors, making it as unique as your fingerprint. Your voice is one of a kind. No one else sounds exactly like you, which is why voiceprints are used for biometric authentication.

I've identified four key elements that form the foundation of every voiceprint: physiology, idiolect, style and soul.

These four elements reflect the intersection of anatomy, linguistics, expression and energetics. Together they create the unique sonic imprint you leave behind. When you consider the number of variables that shape your voice, you begin to understand how individual you truly are. Yes, out of the 8 billion sound-producing citizens in the world, no one has your precise voiceprint.

Physiology – Anatomical Print

Different bodies produce different voices, think variations in vocal cord size and structure of the throat. Physiology also includes illness, injury and voice disorders. From laryngitis to strep infections and a few raspy mornings hungover, I know the pain of a sore throat! Any change to your vocal mechanism alters your sound.

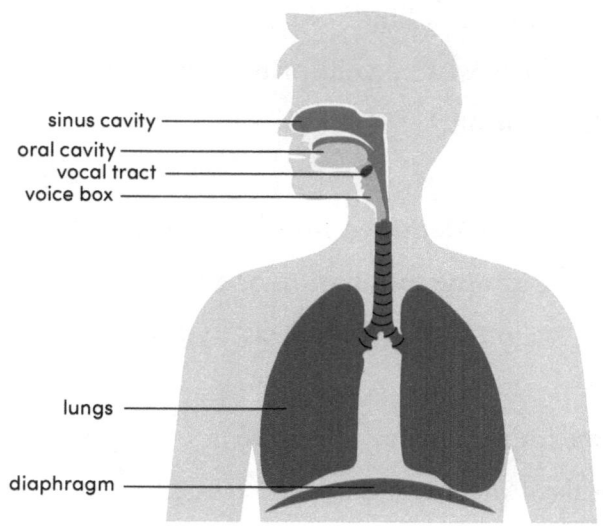

Idiolect – Linguistic Print

Your idiolect is the way you speak thanks to your upbringing, environment and cultural background. It's why someone from New York sounds different to someone from London, and it runs deeper than your accent. You speak a certain language in a certain way largely because of where you grew up and what voices were around you.

I grew up in Wollongong, south of Sydney, Australia – a town affectionately nicknamed The Gong. Even though I haven't lived there in over a decade, I'll often say something to prompt my partner Patrick to joke that, "You can take the girl out of The Gong, but you can't take The Gong out of the girl." As a voice coach, there's something poetic about not being able to take the *gong* out of the girl! No matter where you are now, your voice carries traces of your past.

Style – Expression Print

This is how you express yourself, including tone, pacing, articulation and how you adapt your voice to different situations. Whether you're leading a meeting, telling a joke or pitching an idea, your style largely determines if people sit up or nod off! And the best part? It's entirely within your control. That's why we'll spend a big chunk of this book refining it. Strap in for Part Two!

Soul – Energetic Print
Your voice is the organ of your soul, which means the essence of *who you are* comes through it. When you speak with authenticity, it leaves an energetic signature. This energetic print is the part of your voice that whispers what words cannot, and resonates in the depths of your being. When people say they 'found their voice', this is usually what they were searching for.

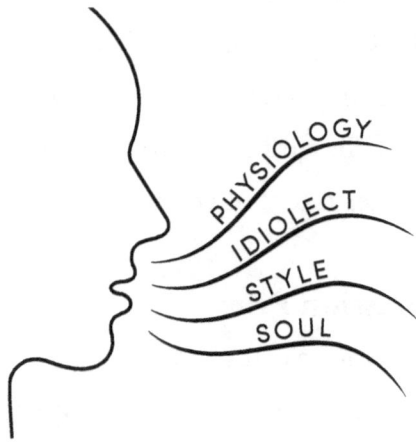

I was going to make these four elements an acronym, but then I realised … I won't be taking the piss in this book. Instead, I'm going to guide you through exactly how to discover, strengthen and own your voiceprint – so you can be memorable, influential and feel incredible when you talk.

Think about the last time you spoke up in a room. Did your voice leave an impression? Was it bold and clear and unmistakably yours? Or was it like that dried-up ink pad in the police station, barely making a mark?

By the end of this book, you won't just speak – you'll leave an imprint that lasts.

"If you don't
claim your voice,
someone else will."

SALLY PROSSER

CHAPTER 2
THE VP BLACK MARKET

"Sorry, but I need to identify you."

Would *you* feel comfortable saying that to the CEO of a major company?

In 2024, that one question saved Ferrari from an expensive scam. It all started with a flurry of WhatsApp messages purporting to be from Ferrari CEO Benedetto Vigna. Let's paraphrase ...

> Hey, did you hear about the big acquisition we're planning?

> I need your help.

> Be ready to sign the non-disclosure agreement our lawyer will send asap.

Then the phone rang, and the voice rang true – complete with Mr Vigna's distinctive southern Italian accent.

According to insiders, the voice was very convincing, but the executive who took the call sensed something was off. A slight oddity in the phrasing. So, he pushed back, asking a question only the real Benedetto knew how to answer.

I can imagine how the conversation went. "Sorry, Benedetto, but I need to identify you. What was the book you recommended to me last week?" The caller immediately hung up, and the deepfake jig was up.[1]

In the same year, actor Scarlett Johansson's voice was hot property for AI. In a statement, she revealed that OpenAI CEO Sam Altman had asked to lend her voice to the system, believing it would be comforting to people who weren't at ease with the technology. She declined. Soon after, OpenAI released a chatbot assistant named Sky. When Johansson heard it, she was stunned. The voice was so close to her own that even friends and journalists thought it was her. The company insisted the voice came from an anonymous actor, yet Sky was pulled when lawyers got involved.[2]

These aren't isolated incidents. Deepfake scams

using face *and* voice are growing exponentially. You've probably seen those eerily lifelike videos of celebrities pushing dodgy crypto schemes. According to a 2024 study by AI firm Sensity, Elon Musk is the most impersonated celebrity in deepfake scams.[3] If this kind of voiceprint scamming can fool Ferrari, frighten Scarlett Johansson, and feature Elon Musk – what hope is there for little old us?

You might think not being rich or famous keeps you safe. Wrong. Even staying off social media won't save your voiceprint from the new black market. No one is immune. AI is rolling in like a freight train – whether you welcome it or not – and taking steps to safeguard your voice will become as commonplace as locking your front door.

In 2025, we're seeing a disturbing rise in scammers voice cloning to:

- Trick parents into thinking their child has been kidnapped
- Manipulate HR professionals into giving up sensitive data
- Deceive small business owners into fraudulent payments

PART ONE

And here's the kicker – it's not about your intelligence; it's about your biology. Hearing a voice, especially a familiar one, activates the limbic system: the emotional control centre of the brain. The stronger the emotional tie, the greater the impact.[4] When the voice belongs to someone you love, it bypasses logic altogether. It's like an audio drug that numbs the rational mind.

That's exactly what happened to Arizona mother Jennifer DeStefano. It was a Friday afternoon in 2023. Her 15-year-old daughter Briana was away on a ski trip when Jennifer got a call from an unknown number. She wouldn't normally pick up.

"Hello?"

What she heard made her blood run cold. It was Briana, sobbing uncontrollably. "Mom, I messed up."

Jennifer reacted instinctively, "Okay, what happened?"

Then came every parent's worst nightmare.

"Mom, these bad men have me. Help me! Help me!" Briana begged and pleaded as the phone was ripped away.

A man's voice snarled, "Listen here, I have your daughter. You tell anyone, you call the cops, I am going to pump her stomach full of drugs, I am going to have my way with her, drop her in Mexico and you'll never see her again."

All the while, Briana screamed in the background, "Mom, help me!"

After a whirlwind of panic, including a $1 million ransom demand, a desperate 911 call, and a frantic attempt to reach Briana – the terrifying 'kidnapping' was revealed to be a high-tech hoax.

"I didn't believe this was a scam," Jennifer later told a US Senate hearing. "It wasn't just Brie's voice, it was *her* cries, it was *her* sobs."[5]

The call ended. But the trauma endured.

And it's only getting more sophisticated. Experts agree you can create a convincing voice clone with less than a minute of audio. Some say it takes just a few seconds.[6]

**So, how do you verify that
someone's voice is really theirs?**

The topic came up in conversation with my sister during sunset snacks on her back deck.

"Sal, you put your whole life online!" she said playfully, plucking an olive.

PART ONE

I chomped my twiggy stick, mentally scrolling through life events in search of something you *couldn't* scroll on a social media feed. *Hmmm.* Between social media, emails, voice messages and all the companies that harbour my data, AI could pull up my past way faster than *I* could!

"I know!" The analogue light bulb dinged in my head. "You could ask me what wild story *that* boyfriend told at *that* Christmas lunch!" I doubt even AI could keep pace with my dating history. We laughed.

But voice security is no laughing matter. "I heard it with my own ears" doesn't hold up in the age of AI – even when it's a familiar voice on the line.

If we want to protect our human technology – our *organic* voice – we need to get serious about securing our voiceprint.

Because soon, "Can you prove it's really you?" won't be a rude question; it'll be standard protocol.

> **EXERCISE**
> **Voice Verification Challenge**
>
> 1. Come up with a question *only your inner circle* would know how to answer.
>
> 2. Test it with a loved one.

You could also come up with a secret passphrase or safe word to escape the bondage of voice fraud and beat the bots at their own game.

Let's be clear. This isn't a manual for avoiding voice scams. I'm sharing this to help you comprehend the immense value of your voice. If strangers view your voice as a goldmine, imagine what it's worth to you.

Your voice is more than sound. It's power. It's identity. It's currency ripe for theft. And it's uniquely yours.

If you don't claim it, someone else might.

So, if the thought of other people or machines running rogue with your voice makes you squirm, it's time to step up and protect it. It's time to put a stake in the ground, or as I like to say – a stake in your sound.

"Your voice is meant
to be expressed,
not suppressed."

SALLY PROSSER

CHAPTER 3
PUT A STAKE IN YOUR SOUND

"Hold still, this will feel a little strange."

The ear, nose and throat specialist snaked the cold camera up my nostril triggering an involuntary shudder. My eyes watered as the foreign object reached the back of my throat to hang in perfect view of my vocal cords. I felt like sneezing, crying and gagging all at the same time. (This ordeal is why the universe spared me from ever needing a COVID-19 test, I like to believe.)

"Ah, see that?"

I blushed. I was a teenager and felt like I was looking at pornography on the doctor's screen (you'll know what I mean if you google 'vocal cords while singing'.)

Mum took me to the specialist due to recurring sore

throat issues. A serious crisis when you're a musical theatre, choir and speech and drama kid. The last straw was having to pull out of the local eisteddfod, for which I'd rehearsed relentlessly.

"See that little pool of mucus?" The doctor looked excited. I looked white. The whole thing was pretty gross, so I just nodded. The remedy was to cut back on dairy. That seemed to fix things, and I was back on stage in a jiffy.

At the time, I thought that was the worst way to lose my voice – physically muted by mucus. I had no idea the most profound silence wouldn't be caused by a physical block at all.

Fast forward to my late 20s. By day, I was a confident TV news reporter, broadcasting my voice across the state. By night, I barely even *had* a voice.

I was in a relationship where I felt like I was walking on eggshells. Of course, I was initially walking on cloud nine. A smart, handsome doctor I met through a friend. We were crazy about each other.

One Tuesday evening I walked into my apartment, and the living room had been transformed. Tea light candles all the way along the wall up onto the TV cabinet and along the sash windowsill. There was a plush blanket and pillows draped on the floor with a beautiful cheese platter and bottle of champagne. This was no occasion. It was the kind of everyday romance I experienced. So, it was a real shock when the cracks began to show.

Things weren't adding up. Money would appear one minute, vanish the next. The drinking got heavier, his mood more erratic, and it turned out this dashing doctor wasn't all that dashing, and it was doubtful he was even a doctor.

I felt so confused. My questions to him were shut down. My words were twisted and thrown back at me. Self-trust evaporated, and my voice began to retreat.

I never saw proof of him being a doctor. No record at the university. No record at the hospital. The document I asked him to provide as proof of employment, I later found under the lid of my printer – a cobbled-together sticky-tape and liquid-paper arts and craft job.

He later told me all this confusion was because he was in witness protection and worked for a national intelligence agency. As you can imagine, that really cleared things up for me. Before *Voiceprint* came along, my book was going to be titled *The Spy Who Shagged Me*.

PART ONE

You can laugh. It is funny.

What's funnier is I believed him and I stood by him. I got to a point where I didn't care who the hell he was or what he did, or even if he was truthful about it – because I loved him and wanted to be with him. And I wanted to be right. I didn't want to admit to myself that I'd got it so wrong.

Family members weren't quite so sympathetic. They were on the futile warpath to help me see the truth. So, I did what any love-blind woman in my situation would do: told my family we broke up and continued to date him in secret.

I was the keeper of lies. I couldn't keep track of them and felt so ashamed of the whole thing. The lie-addiction crash was real. Swept up in the exhausting love-bomb cycle of highs and lows, I withdrew from everyone, and my voice withdrew from me.

I'd look at him across the room, lost in his dark features, and tell myself, *This is love. This is worth it. Love means standing by someone no matter what.* But deep down, a truer voice whispered that something was wrong.

One night, that voice of doubt found the courage to come out in the messy way it does. He didn't like it. Dislike quickly turned to danger, fuelled by his drunkenness. He chased me down the hallway into the bedroom with the four points of an upturned chair before kicking me in the thigh, sending me onto the bed. *Why didn't I scream, or at least say something?* My voice dove back to the safety of silence, and I was paralysed. Frozen in fear.

My body was pinned to the mattress by an invisible weight of guilt and grief and shame and anger. *How did an educated, privileged woman like me get herself into this shit? What a fucking idiotic disappointment to society.* The self-loathing pummelled and crushed me against rock bottom.

The next morning, he was gone.

I hadn't moved.

Morning sunlight beamed through the shutters with a joy I yearned to feel. Lying there, drunk on a cocktail of crappy emotions, something stirred in my belly. The sensation was hot and otherworldly. I took a deep, low breath in … and as I exhaled, I felt that fiery sensation rise up my windpipe, past my vocal cords and out my mouth. The guttural wail took on a life of its own.

It wasn't a scream. It was a sound forged in the depths

of my being – primal, raw and undeniable. As it surged up through my body, it didn't just echo in the empty apartment; it echoed through me. I felt it reverberate in my bones, in my throat, in every space where my voice had once been swallowed.

In that moment, I knew I was done being silent.
In that moment, I reclaimed the voice I knew I had.
In that moment, I put a stake in my sound.

I realised there's a big difference between speaking with confidence and speaking your truth. And I realised my life's mission was to help people find their inner fire and channel it through their soul-stirring voice.

So, I ask you, have you put a stake in your sound?

Have you ever had an FMV moment? A *FIND MY VOICE* moment? A moment when you could no longer hold your tongue and finally spoke your truth.

A moment when you courageously:

- Broke the seal of secrecy and revealed, "I need help" or, "I'm gay" or, "I want a divorce."
- Dropped the mask and expressed your creativity, for example, through singing, stand-up comedy or reading poetry to an audience.
- Voiced your opinion in a big meeting, asked your boss for a pay raise, or handed in your resignation.
- Reclaimed your story and refused to let others twist the narrative.
- Hit post on a vulnerable video or raised your hand to grab the mic.
- Spoke up for someone who didn't have a voice and, in doing so, found your own.
- Took a chance with phrases like, "I love you" or, "I'm sorry" or, "I forgive you."

A moment when, at last, your voice caught up to what your head and heart had always known.

Maybe you've forgotten your FMV. Maybe reading this book *is* that moment for you. Maybe you've just been waiting for someone to say: you're allowed.

So, here it is, your permission slip. Make the declaration. Say it aloud, whisper it if you must, but say it: "My voice will be expressed, not suppressed."

Your voice is the soundtrack of who you are, the organ of your soul.

The disclaimer I often share is that I can't *fix* your voice and I can't *give* you a better voice, but as a voice coach, I *can* help you release your own. And releasing your own voice, the soul element of your voiceprint, begins with identifying Your Reason to Speak. You may have heard the quote: "When the why is clear, the how is easy." I'd add to that: when the why is clear, the voice *flows easy.*

When you know Your Reason to Speak, you tap into the beautiful relief of your soul resonance, and it's like a vocal homecoming. It reminds me of that scene in *The Lion King* where Simba is staring into his reflection in the river when it morphs into his father, Mufasa, and we hear the haunting words, "Simbaaaa, remember who you are …"

EXERCISE
Your Reason to Speak

Step 1: Connect with your voice element

What element in nature inspires you to speak? Go with your first instinct, even if it feels random or unusual, and be specific.
For example, if you choose water – is it a rolling wave? Ocean mist? Cracking ice? The first drop of rain? A clear lake?
A waterfall? Have the picture in your mind.

For me, it's fire, specifically when it's burning like a torch you can hold.

Step 2: Extract the element's wisdom

What qualities of this natural force are you drawn to? Describe it – is it soft or powerful? Steady or surprising? Does it invite, challenge, ground, stir, refresh?

I love how fire is so bright and dynamic. The flames dance, ignite and grow. You only need one candle to light another – and soon, *boom*, the whole room is bright!

Step 3: Know who you're here to impact

Who does your voice serve? These are the

people you're here to move. Be specific. Are they women in leadership, creators, sensitive souls, founders, teens or educators?

My programs are designed for heart-led business owners and professionals.

Step 4: Identify the transformation your voice delivers

What is the shift or change your voice is here to create? What becomes available when people truly hear you? What do you help others become or do? Instead of focusing on the pain or the problem, think about the solution and use positive language.

The transformation my voice delivers takes people from fearing public speaking and neglecting their voice to speaking with confidence and loving how they sound.

Step 5: Define the ripple effect

What becomes possible for people after experiencing your voice? Why does Step 4 matter? Go beyond surface-level wins. What soul-shift or empowerment becomes possible?

There are *so* many benefits of valuing your voice and speaking with confidence. At the heart of it, the world will benefit from the impact of your message – and you'll feel great about it!

Now weave it all together

I am [Step 1] who is [Step 2]. My voice helps [Step 3] to [Step 4] so they can [Step 5].

My example:

I am a burning torch who is bright and leads the way. My voice helps ignite the fire in business owners and professionals to speak with confidence so they can light up the world with their voice and feel great about it!

Examples from clients:

"I am a tall, proud tree who holds my ground and accepts who I am. My voice helps mothers shift their thinking so they can connect with who they are and live their soul's purpose and desire." – Emma.

"I am a warm campfire who is dynamic and comforting. My voice helps indigenous communities have access to safe, clean drinking water so they can live a healthy secure life while maintaining connection to Country." – Karen.

"I am a free-flowing river whose voice nourishes those around me to help them feel valued so they're excited to come to work and contribute." – Jo.

PART ONE

Let Your Reason to Speak be your energetic anchor – grounding you as you walk into your next meeting, share your next idea or post your next social media video. Awaken the memory of your FMV moment, remember who you are and speak from a place that's aligned, authentic and deeply rooted in purpose.

"When the why is clear,
the voice flows easy."

SALLY PROSSER

"Don't conform to the sound of society. Pioneer the sound of yourself."

SALLY PROSSER

CHAPTER 4
OPERATION VOICE CUPID

If you look real close at the inside of my office door, you'll see them.

Scratch marks.

I don't have a cat or a puppy.

However, I have had many a client want to claw their way out in horror at the sound of their voice played back. Maybe you can relate.

Do you hate the sound of your voice?
The speed with which you answer *yes* to that question is telling! When I said, "Put a stake in your sound," I didn't mean stab the metaphoric love-heart cake of your voice. I was thinking more cupid-style. By the end of

this chapter, you'll be wining and dining your voice like the soulmate you forgot you had.

Why don't you love the sound of your voice?
If you cringe when you hear your voice on a recording, you're not alone. It's such a common phenomenon it has a name – voice confrontation.[7]

You sound different to yourself when you're speaking compared to hearing your voice played back.
You know how your voice sounds good in the shower? Well, when you hear yourself speaking in real-time, it's like a built-in shower voice because you're hearing the vibrations through your skull. It's called bone conduction, which gives your voice a deeper, richer, warmer quality. When you hear your voice on a recording, it's through air conduction – the sound waves leave the speaker, travel through the air and are picked up by your ears. It sounds higher, thinner and unfamiliar.

Hearing your voice on a recording can be a psychological shock.

Your brain has created an identity around how you *think* you sound. When you hear a recording that doesn't match your internal perception, it feels off. There's a term I use for this disconnect beyond just a fleeting cringe. I call it vocal dysmorphia.

Negative self-judgement festers because our voice is so deeply tied to our identity. Think about all four elements of your voiceprint – physiology, idiolect, style and soul. If your voice doesn't align with how you want to be seen and heard, you'll instinctively reject it. When listening to a recording, you become hyperaware of every little imperfection, especially if you tend to be your own worst critic.

How many times have you recorded a voicemail and rerecorded it ten times because you 'sounded weird'? Or how often did you decide *not* to post a video because you didn't like your voice? "Ew, do I really sound like that?" is a common complaint I hear from clients. "Can you fix it?"

PART ONE

> **Here's the truth:**
> **Your voice doesn't need fixing.**
> **It needs friendship.**

So yes, clients may *want* to claw their way out of my office, but I do my job and hold them hostage to their voice-hate until they release it.

> **Not only *can* you learn to**
> **love your voice – you must.**

If you want your voice to *leave* a positive impression when you speak, you need to *hold* a positive impression of your voice. Imagine if you physically cringed and recoiled every time you saw a friend. They'd probably ghost you, and they certainly wouldn't come to your aid in times of need. Your voice is the same. Show it compassion, understanding, love and appreciation – and it will be there for you. You'll enjoy each other's company, and your energy will show it.

How do you get to that point?

Start with a date and let the love for your voice blossom. **Familiarity builds fondness.**

> **EXERCISE**
> **Operation Voice Cupid**
>
> **Step 1: Record yourself in a safe space**
> Record a podcast or social media video or read a short passage from this book – you can even voice record your shopping list onto your phone. The content doesn't matter.
>
> **Step 2: Listen with curiosity, not judgement**
> Play back the recording and listen as if you're hearing a friend, like it's not *your* voice. Notice what you like and simply observe what you don't.
>
> And that's it! Repeat often.
>
> **If you cringe – persist!**

Writer and creator Erica Mallett coined a brilliant concept – Cringe Mountain. You have to climb it if you want to get good at anything.[8] Here's my definition:

> Cringe Mountain (n.):
> The steep psychological hill you must climb to be at peace with your own voice.

PART ONE

I cringe big time when I hear my old radio and TV news reports. I cringe when I listen to single-digit episodes of *That Voice Podcast* – and don't even mention my early TikToks. I was trekking up Cringe Mountain on that platform long before the term was invented!

If I retreated at the first cringe, I would not have had a successful career as a journalist and released 250+ episodes of my podcast, and I certainly never would have grown a community of 500K+ on social media, or published this book for that matter.

I still have family and friends tell me: "Sal, you're so cringe." One said I personified "brand cringe." This may have stung before I did so much personal development work. Now it just means I'm doing something right. Truly learning to love your voice and putting it out there is an inside job.

Your voice is an integral part of who you are.

Healing your relationship with your voice is healing your relationship with your greatest love – yourself. And if this concept brings up a bit of sick in your mouth, let me ask you this – who has a speaking voice you really love? Maybe Morgan Freeman or David Attenborough? Perhaps Kate Winslet or Meryl Streep is more your sound?

Would you swap voices with them if given the chance?

Freaky Friday style. *Poof!* One morning you sound exactly like that person.

Really, would you? Most people I've asked/held hostage in my office say no. Even clients who were initially adamant they hated their voice end up admitting that giving it away would be like stripping out part of their soul.

> **Your voice is as unique as your fingerprint.**
> **It's not to be traded, copied or forced into**
> **a box that sounds like everyone else.**

Here's the twist: even if you wouldn't swap voices on purpose, you may already be doing it without realising. Have you noticed people starting to sound the same? Maybe it's your kids parroting their friends or your partner picking up phrases from colleagues.

This phenomenon is called the chameleon effect.

We subconsciously mimic the voices around us – their speech patterns, inflections and pace – to foster stronger social bonds and feel like we belong.[9]

After living in the UK for a year, I came home weirdly and frequently saying, "Bless," just like my Londoner friend. Harmless and kind of cute. Patrick drops a lot more f-bombs after hanging out at the bike club. I jokingly call that the Harley effect.

It raises an important question: When are you adapting, and when are you abandoning the voice that's truly yours?
The scary thing is that the chameleon effect can take effect almost straight away. Your voice is constantly setting the tone for the people around you, and they're setting the tone for you. Is this a tone you want to amplify? If you're not proud of your unique voiceprint, at worst you'll speak from the *wrong* song sheet, and at best you'll speak from the *same* song sheet as everyone else.

> **Why conform to the sound of society when you can pioneer the sound of yourself?**

Courageously pioneer the expedition right up Cringe Mountain! And when you reach the summit, take your voice on a romantic date. Just don't be surprised if it turns into a chaotic polygamous affair. We rarely bring only *one* voice to the table. A whole chorus of inner critics, impostors, judges, perfectionists and people pleasers often drown out the one true voice we need to hear.

That's why, sometimes, the most strategic move isn't to speak louder – it's to go quiet.

"A pounding heart before speaking is much better than no heartbeat at all!"

SALLY PROSSER

CHAPTER 5
GO QUIET TO BE HEARD

"Any last words?"

My eyes darted around the room searching for support. They caught the big brown eyes of a woman wearing a beanie. We'd only met minutes before, but in that moment, we became comrades. Soul sisters with a shared apprehension.

"We're all good then?" The voice of the retreat leader, Kara, broke our eye contact.

And so, it began.

Thirty-six hours of complete silence.

No talking. No pointing. No charades-style acting. And no eye contact. My pupil-pash with the brown-eyed woman was over.

PART ONE

Our group of 12 filed silently into the dining room and sat at a long table shoulder to shoulder.

Dinner is served.

The ideal choice for eating in silence … SOUP! *Bloody hell. How's this going to work?*

To my right – the brown-eyed woman pulled her beanie down like she knew I'd struggle not to violate the rules. To my left – a blondish woman wearing a pink jacket was barely keeping it together. I was hungry, and a TikTok tutorial about how to politely eat soup came far too late for this experience.

I wasn't game to start.

From across the table, a leader emerged with a faint slurp. Pink Jacket couldn't contain her laughter and snorted in a futile effort to hold it in. I closed my eyes and visualised coffins and dead puppies in an attempt to maintain decorum. *Breathe, Sal. Don't be immature. You're on this silent retreat to find yourself.*

After staring into the soup for another few seconds, I took the spoon and dived in.

That retreat in 2021 was the beginning of my foray into silent experiences. A speaking coach's quiet quest to calm the inner voices. The Soup Saga was a walk in the park compared to the 10-day Vipassana meditation course I took in remote England. That was seriously hardcore hushing. On top of the no talking, there was also no reading, no writing, no exercise and no dinner. Oh, and 11 hours of meditation every day.

"Sal, why in the world did you put yourself through that?!" My high-school mate sounded genuinely concerned on the phone. I *had* been crying my eyes out on Instagram – and considering my videos are normally as animated as a kid's TV show, it was a shock to the @sallyprosservoice system.

In the peace of writing this chapter, I wished I'd responded to my friend with something like: "If you can't spend time truly listening to your inner voices, how will you ever know your physical voice is flowing to its full potential?"

Let's be real, in the moment, I said, "I have no fucking idea." Then slugged my room service red wine and binged *Emily in Paris*.

Those 10 days really knocked me for six. Maybe I'm too auditory; maybe I'm too restless, and clearly – I wasn't ready for it.

While I would issue a warning before venturing on

Vipassana, I would highly recommend escaping the noise of everyday life to hear your true inner voice.

From the chatter of social media and dinging of inboxes to the loud opinions of know-it-alls and advice from the well-meaning brigade to the podcasts and playlists – the inner voice of who you are and what you truly want doesn't stand a chance.

> **Forget drowning out the noise, go somewhere you can switch it off altogether.**

If you dare to stop and listen, really listen, you might just meet the version of yourself you've been too busy to hear. And you might just encounter the speaking story that's *really* been holding your voice back.

What's your speaking story?

The problem is people are obsessed with who they were yesterday. Tony Robbins introduced me to that concept, and it has sat in my brain like an earworm.

It's so true. We're programmed from birth with stories of how to live and who to be. Most of our adult life is spent re-acting the patterns we learnt in childhood.

Shut up. Be a good girl and be quiet. Shh! The adults are talking. Nobody cares what you think. That's a dumb question. Speak properly! You're too loud. You're so dramatic. You talk too much.

These are common speaking stories I uncover with my clients. Some might resonate with you.

Often the scenario is:
- Getting laughed at when speaking up at school or university.
- Being ignored when sharing your idea – and then watching someone else repeat the idea and get credit.
- Being interrupted constantly.
- Experiencing a perceived public speaking flop.
- Having a strict 'seen and not heard' upbringing, learning silence equals safety.
- Being bullied for your voice – your accent, pitch, tone or pronunciation.
- Not feeling like you can 'win'. For example, as a woman, being told you "sound like a girl" is usually levelled as an insult and so is "you sound like a man."
- A teacher or authority figure shutting you down

PART ONE

and making you feel unworthy of being heard.

In times of stress or overwhelming emotions, these past experiences literally come to the tip of your tongue. Clients describe their voice seizing or wavering as though they were smack-bang back in that voice-blocking memory. It's vocal regression – a psychological defence mechanism where a person reverts to an earlier stage of emotional development as a way to cope.

Maybe you've experienced falling into the speaking style of a younger version of yourself in certain settings or around certain people? Those are vocal regression triggers.

One of my clients, we'll call Paul, is a successful entrepreneur who came to me because his voice didn't match his credentials and people weren't listening to him. Paul physically spoke down towards the ground, struggled to articulate his thoughts, and complained of a block he couldn't put his finger on.

Upon deeper exploration, we unearthed the root of the problem: Paul didn't feel safe to be heard because his voice was essentially trapped in the 7-year-old version of himself – a little boy who had learnt that speaking up could lead to punishment. His earliest memory was asking his father for a glass of water, only to have it flung in his face with the loveless shout: "Get it your damn self!" Paul ran, soaked and shaken, back to his bedroom – vocally scarred.

By identifying this origin, we were able to release his voice using vocal and somatic (body-focused) techniques. Today, Paul speaks with confidence and ease in rooms all over the world.

Is a false narrative throwing you off your voiceprint?

It's impossible to have a strong voiceprint if the soundtrack playing on repeat in your mind is working against you. And it's impossible to rewrite the story if you don't know what's already on the page.

EXERCISE
This Means That

Complete the following phrases with the first thing that comes to mind.

1. A pounding heart before speaking means

   _____

2. If I can't answer a question, that means

   _____

3. My last speech flopped, so that means my next speech will

   _____

4. Stumbling over my words means

   _____

5. Being interrupted in a meeting means

   _____

If the story isn't helpful, rewrite it. Reframe it.

For example, a pounding heart before speaking *could* mean you're super nervous and bound to screw things up. Who's that story helping? A pounding heart before speaking could mean your heart is cheering for you. I mean, a pounding heart is a lot better than no heartbeat at all! It means you're *alive*! Nerves and excitement actually feel the same in the body. *You* get to assign the meaning. People often ask me if I get nervous before speaking – like it's a bad thing. I say, "Absolutely, *yes* I get nervous, and I love the feeling!" Stress isn't inherently negative.

Harvard University did an incredible study called 'Mind over Matter'. In part one, participants had to give a 5-minute impromptu speech on their personal weaknesses to two judges trained to give snarky non-verbal feedback, like crossing their arms. *Sounds like a special kind of hell, right?* For a words-person like me, part two of the experiment was where it got terrifying. It was a math test. You had to count backwards in steps of 7 from 996, while the evaluators heckled. *Stress-ful!*

All the participants were stressed, but only *half* the participants were instructed to see the signs of stress as their body helping them meet the challenge. Just like the pounding heart cheering for them, the fast breathing meant more oxygen to their brain. Every symptom of stress was reframed to be helpful.

These participants were not only less anxious and more confident, incredibly their physical stress response changed. In a typical stress response, the blood vessels constrict – one of the reasons chronic stress is sometimes associated with cardiovascular disease. But in the study, the blood vessels of the participants who saw their stress as a good thing stayed relaxed. So, the science shows that it's not the stress itself; it's how you *think* about stress.[10]

If you're stuck on the This Means That exercise, DM me on social media for an idea, or just fill out the prompts with: *Whatever I want it to mean!*

Our thoughts can be gremlins or gifts.

Things mean whatever we choose them to mean. And that choice impacts the way we show up and the voice we use. When you uncover your speaking story and flip unhelpful thoughts into trusted allies, you unlock a powerful shift.

Whoa, I can feel it.

IDENTIFY YOUR VOICEPRINT

You've survived the noise – and the silence! You've rewritten the story. Now, it's time to breathe new life into your voice.

"Oxygen powers your voice. Without breath there is no voice."

SALLY PROSSER

CHAPTER 6
GROUND AND BREATHE

"Who wants more?"

I looked around the group, and several people shook their heads. I cautiously raised my hand.

"Okay great, let's go," said Leah, our tour leader.

Everyone piled into four-wheel drives, and we took a gorgeous journey through the snow-covered mountains of Thredbo, Australia. As we pulled into a small car park, my heart rate rose.

The moment I stepped out, the winter air engulfed me, and snowflakes caught on my eyelashes. I made the ominous trudge down the slippery embankment towards the river.

This was it. No time to hesitate. Boots off, socks off,

jacket off, pants off, beanie off. I slipped and slid my little white butt into the water. It was near freezing, and I swore like a sailor being chucked overboard.

"*Fuuuuck!!*"

It felt like a thousand knives were piercing my skin.

"Breathe, Sal, you've got this. Just breathe." Leah's voice was calm and strong.

I closed my eyes and focused on her voice.

"Breathe. Just breathe."

With each inhale, I felt warmth course through my body. With each exhale, I let myself sink deeper into the water. I was centred. I was focused. I was bizarrely comfortable.

Then before I knew it, "Okay, that's time. Everyone out!"

Back by the fire at the chalet, I reflected on what I'd just done – plunged into an icy river and breathed my way to comfort. *Like, seriously?!* I'm a high-heel-wearing, inner-city Pilates-goer who sports long nails and had barely taken a cold shower before that long weekend in the Snowy Mountains.

The Wim Hof Method is truly incredible. It's a breathing, cold exposure and mindset training technique developed by Wim Hof, a Dutchman known as 'The Iceman'. I embarked on the experience to understand more about the power of breath control. And to overcome my fear of the cold.

You see, I was born on an unseasonably hot Friday in October, and Mum told me that's why I was a 'cold' baby she had to rug up. Just like a speaking story, that temperature story ran deep. I always took a cardigan when I went out, even in summer, and carried a crochet blanket to drape over my legs on school bus excursions. Yes, I was like a teenage granny. My friends called me Margaret – the most old-fashioned name they could think of at the time.

This chilling background story made my dip in the near freezing Thredbo River all the more challenging. It was a huge personal breakthrough and armed me with way more than a heightened appreciation for a hot shower.

Public speaking can feel like plunging into subzero temperatures – especially if the audience gives you a frosty reception! And just as you can breathe through the cold, guess what? **You can breathe through public speaking anxiety.**

PART ONE

When you exhale longer than you inhale, *boom*, you activate the vagus nerve – the superhighway of the parasympathetic nervous system, which runs from the brain stem right down to the abdomen.[11] I call it the Las Vegas nerve because it parties all over the body, lighting up a signal to regulate your senses.

Deep breathing to calm anxiety isn't a revelation. The real revelation is *how* you breathe and *why* it's critical to the way you speak. If the only time you think about breathing is when you're feeling stressed, you are missing a trick – or 22,000. Yep, we take on average 22,000 breaths every day.[12] How many of these breaths do you notice?

Notice a breath now.
Inhale. Exhale.

The secret to a stronger voice is at the tip of your nose.

Why have we forgotten how to breathe? We weren't born this way. Picture a crying baby. Their whole torso is expanding and contracting. It's pure voice. It's why such big sounds emerge from such tiny humans. As we grow up, we can lose that natural voice we had as babies. Maybe, like I mentioned in the last chapter, you were told to "shut up" or "suck it in" or "stand there and look pretty."

Maybe over time your diaphragm locked, your breathing shallowed and your voice weakened. And just because you don't *think* about breathing, doesn't mean you're breathing effectively, let alone optimally.

> Breathing isn't natural;
> it's habitual.

What breathing habits have you formed?
Put your hand on your tummy and breathe in. What direction did your hand move? If it moved in or up, chances are you're breathing high into the top cones of your lungs. If your hand moved out, you're filling the depths of your lungs – which is fab for speaking.

> Oxygen powers your voice.
> Without breath there is no voice.

PART ONE

If human voices were in the orchestra, we'd be in the woodwind section – powered by air. And just like a musical instrument, you need to hold it correctly before you start playing. How do you hold your voice?

Better question: Where is your voice?
Your throat? Your mouth? Your head?

All are correct – and all are not the full story. Speaking is a whole-of-body experience (not to be confused with an out-of-body experience lol). Your voice is a powerful energetic channel that runs from the soles of your feet to the crown of your head – and beyond. And freaking out before speaking always presents as physical symptoms.

Your body can feel like a zoo. The ants are running up your legs; the butterflies are loose in your tummy; the gorillas are having a fist fight in your chest; the boa constrictor is wrapped around your neck, and the hyperactive monkey is chattering away in your head.

In that moment, I recommend getting out of your head and into your body via a Body Scan.

EXERCISE
Body Scan

1. Feet: Are they grounded and strong? Wiggle your toes, stretch your ankles and shoot imaginary tree roots down into the floor below.

2. Knees: Are they unlocked? Shake out your legs. First from the knees, then from the hips.

3. Belly: Is it fired up and ready to go? Swirl your hips like you're a professional hula-hooper.

4. Shoulders: Are they back and strong? Roll your shoulders forward and backward, then bounce them up and down. Imagine you're wearing big angel wings, and draw the shoulders back and down.

5. Neck and head: Are they relaxed and in line with your spine? Gently stretch your neck side to side. Imagine a magnetic string pulling your head up to the ceiling. Acting like a meerkat looking over grassland works here.

6. Face: Is your smile lighting up your eyes? Give your temples and cheeks a gentle massage, and smile – it's a great time to be alive!

7. Repeat as needed.

PART ONE

Now that you're grounded and *in* your physical body, you can draw on the energetic field around you.

To help explain, let me take you back to the Sydney 2000 Olympics. The crowd erupted as fan favourite, Indigenous athlete Cathy Freeman launched out of the blocks in the final of the 400 m. Dressed in the iconic green, gold and white suit, she came around the bend for the final stretch. Cathy was in third place with 80 metres to go. Her description of the event gives me chills every time I hear it. No icy river needed.

"This is my moment. I feel like I'm being protected. My ancestors were the first people to walk on this land. It's a really powerful force.

For the first time I feel the stadium. I feel the people, I feel their energy. I feel like I'm being carried and know exactly what I need to do.

I can win this. I *will* win this."[13]

And she did. It was one of the greatest moments in Australian Olympic history.

IDENTIFY YOUR VOICEPRINT

When the spotlight is on you and the vehicle for your message is your voice – don't think for a second you're on your own.

Like Cathy Freeman, you can always tap into the energy around you and channel it through you. You don't need to be an Olympic athlete to feel that wonderful paradox of being securely connected to the earth and simultaneously free to fly.

Every time you speak, your breath carries your ancestors, your energy, your intention.

PART ONE

Look at it through the chakra lens.

Our chakras are energetic centres that govern the flow of life force within us. Your voice runs through all of them – not just the throat.

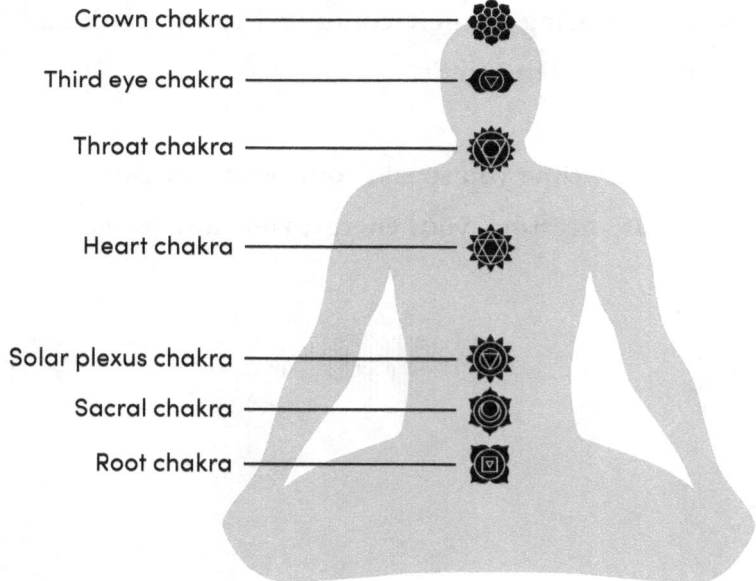

IDENTIFY YOUR VOICEPRINT

EXERCISE
Chakra Voice Check-In

Breathe into the corresponding chakra as you say the following affirmations on the exhale:

CROWN (higher knowing/top of head)
Words flow to me freely and easily

THIRD EYE (intuition/between your eyes)
I see the impact I want to have

THROAT (communication/throat)
My voice is a channel for self-expression

HEART (passion/chest)
I love sharing my voice with the audience

SOLAR PLEXUS (self-esteem/upper abdomen)
My voice deserves to be heard

SACRAL (pleasure/lower belly)
I get such a buzz out of speaking

ROOT (foundation/lower back)
I am standing in my power

This energetic chain forms a channel for your breath, which fuels your voice.

In many languages, the word for *breath* and *spirit* is the same. For example, *prana* in Sanskrit, *pneuma* in Greek and *ruach* in Hebrew.

While we're geeking out on etymology, the word *inspiration* comes from the Latin *inspirare,* which means 'to breathe in'. Every time you breathe in, you are inspiring yourself – you are giving spirit to your words.

> **Physically and spiritually, you cannot
> inspire others with your words if
> you don't first inspire yourself.**

How *should* you breathe?

Send that life force energy to where it's needed most. Do the Body Scan and breathe into any points of tension. You can also breathe into whatever chakra you feel called to nourish. Breath is nature's great elixir and cleanser; it moves energy and emotions through the body.

When you feel anxious, your body tends to tense up – especially through the chest, neck and shoulders – and this squeezes the air up like you're a tube of toothpaste. This, in turn, squeezes the voice up, which is why when you're nervous your voice can pop into a pitch only dogs and small children can hear.

Decreased airflow can also result in a creaky, crackly sound known as 'vocal fry'. It got the name because it sounds like something sizzling in a frying pan. People often dip into fry at the ends of sentences, so I work with clients to let their breath flow from one end of a sentence all the way to the other.

Now, I'm not here to be the vocal fry police – and I fully acknowledge that women, in particular, are unfairly judged for using it. So don't get rid of your vocal fry for others – do it for *yourself*. Vocal fry is a sign of poor breath flow and lack of support. Not only is breath the currency of connection, it's also the oil for vocal health. In other words, vocal fry will eventually fry your vocal cords.

As a general rule, breathing low and deep into the body will help counteract this. Imagine your buttocks are your lungs. (Just note: breathe *in* to your bottom, not *out* – that's a lasting impression you'd rather not leave.) You want the air to be deep enough to naturally engage your diaphragm.

PART ONE

Diamonds aren't a girl's best friend; the diaphragm's a girl's best friend.

Start training it! Because if your D is in play, your voice leads the way.

Your diaphragm is like a parachute, saving you from a speaking freefall. When you inhale, your diaphragm expands downward like an opening parachute, and when you exhale, it relaxes back up, just like a parachute deflates as it lands. The dome-shaped muscles and tendons run under your lungs and around to your lower back. It's the main breathing muscle and lives in the home of our solar plexus chakra – the seat of our self-esteem and self-belief. Is it any wonder why when we doubt ourselves, the diaphragm locks up and we lose control over our voice?

Strengthen your diaphragm with an exercise I call The Angry Librarian.

> ## **EXERCISE**
> ### The Angry Librarian
>
> - Take a breath in low and deep and as you exhale say: "Sh! Sh! Shhhhhh!"
>
> - On each pulse, feel your diaphragm (the muscle just below your sternum) push in towards your spine each time.
>
> - On the last "shhhhhh," keep going until you release all the air in your body. Your lungs will feel like shrivelled sultanas.
>
> - Then when you can't hold any more, relax and enjoy the satisfying new breath in. It should dive right down low in your body.

Your sound is sabotaged or supported before it's even made.

Your voiceprint takes form long before the vocal cords vibrate.

When you feel your voice is failing – breathe.

When you feel your heart rate rise – breathe.

When you feel unsteady on your feet – breathe.

PART ONE

**If you have your breath,
you will have your voice.**

One of my clients, Laetitia, spoke at a big International Women's Day event and, in her words, started "losing it" when she looked out at the hundreds of faces. She threw out her script and led the audience through a Nadi Shodhana, which is an alternate nostril breathing exercise.

"We're going to balance our divine feminine and divine masculine because I need it now and I'm sure you need it as well. So, let's breathe together."

Laetitia felt immediately calmer and more aligned, and everyone in the audience was so present listening to her words. She even had women approach her afterwards praising her for the opening exercise. As a teacher and healer, Laetitia wasn't afraid to admit the exercise wasn't prepared and was grateful she could surrender to her intuitive nudge in that moment to breathe.

I implore you to be like Laetitia.

> **Always surrender to the breath.**
> **Listen to the spirit within you.**

Spiritual teacher Ma Jaya Sati Bhagavati said, "The more you listen to your breath, the more you can hear the voice of your soul."

Remember, you can't breathe in while you're speaking, only while you're pausing. So, stop, ground and connect to yourself. Think on the 'in' breath. Speak on the 'out' breath.

> **Inspire yourself, and your**
> **voice will inspire others.**

And *practise* using the power of your breath. Even if you're not inclined to sit in a snowy river, I'd challenge you to crank the cold in the shower and breathe through 30 seconds. The more you can breathe when your body is in a stressful state, the easier it will be to breathe through any speaking situation – especially when the stakes are high.

PART ONE

By now you know:
- What your voiceprint is
- Why it's worth protecting
- Why your voiceprint matters
- How to love your voice
- How to listen to your inner voice
- How to ground and breathe

Let's settle into your toes now and take a big refreshing breath in for a count of 1, 2, 3, 4, and then a big sigh out for 4, 3, 2, 1.

The prep work is done. The ink pad is fresh. Now you're ready to speak with *style* and truly *impress* with your voiceprint.

PART TWO

IMPRESS WITH YOUR VOICEPRINT

"It's easy to 'wing it' when you've been preparing your whole life."

SALLY PROSSER

CHAPTER 7
THE V.O.I.C.E FORMULA

"Try again. It's left, right, left and slide."

The choreographer's patience was wearing thin.

"Okay, left, right, left and ..." I took a sheepish pause. "What was it again?"

I'd been kept back after rehearsals for a private session with one of the lead dancers. The school musical was *Little Shop of Horrors,* and I was out of my high-achieving comfort zone. I loved performing on stage. Acting? Bring it on. Singing? Passable. Dancing? Well, this is why I was held back. My brain-to-feet-to-arm coordination was not happening. I struggled to mirror the moves; the teachers went too fast for me, and I stuck out like a sore thumb, not a star performer. So, there I was. Dance

Detention. Having my arms and legs manipulated like an old puppet. They had to break it down step by step. And that's exactly how we're going to approach showtime for your voiceprint.

In Part One we established:
- You have a voiceprint.
- It's worth valuing.
- Belief, body and breath form the foundation of your voiceprint.

Now, we go deeper and firmer. *Oh yes, baby!* Part Two explains how to *impress* your audience when you speak.

Have you ever been captivated by a great speaker and wondered, *How do they do it?* Some will tell you they're just going with the flow, completely off-the-cuff. After one presentation, someone asked me how long I'd spent preparing. I smiled and said, "About forty years."

It's easy to *look* like you're winging it when you've been preparing your whole life. Now, I'm about to burst the bluff and reveal the real reason great speakers seem so effortless. It's not magic – it's mechanics. There are simple techniques anyone can learn. And let's face it: **a formula is far more reliable than a fluke.**

Introducing the V.O.I.C.E Formula.

This formula layers-up like each of those dance moves, and if you're just starting out, don't worry about the clunky two-left-feet situation. This isn't about mastering everything at once. If you try to tackle all the elements simultaneously, you may feel like I did in that chorus line – arms and legs flailing in random directions.

Let's take it step by step:

- **V = VIBRATIONS**
  Tune into the frequency of your voice.

- **O = OPENNESS**
  Allow your voice space to flow.

- **I = INTONATION**
  Master the musicality in your voice.

- **C = CLARITY**
  Land every word with precision.

- **E = EXPRESSION**
  Engage and wow your audience.

PART TWO

Each of these layers adds richness, depth and *style* to your voiceprint – regardless of the speaking scenario. Whether you're recording a video, hosting a podcast, leading a meeting, delivering a keynote or even having a D&M with a loved one – the V.O.I.C.E Formula will ensure you leave a lasting impression when you speak.

With practice, patience and perseverance, you'll become the prima ballerina of your voiceprint.

1, 2, 3, 4 – let's begin!

Are you ready for the V.O.I.C.E Formula?

"If you want to find
the secrets of the universe,
think in terms of energy,
frequency and vibration."

NIKOLA TESLA

CHAPTER 8
V = VIBRATIONS

"It's been a long time coming ... It's you and me. That's my whole world. They whisper in the hallway, 'She's a bad, bad girl.'"

The stand was literally shaking. A choir of 96,000 voices filled the famous Melbourne Cricket Ground, conducted by our fearless leader Miss Taylor Alison Swift.

The Eras Tour wasn't a concert. It was a visceral musical experience coded with high-vibrational joy and peace. More than 10 million people felt the energetic pull. Once wasn't enough for me, so I flew from Brisbane to London to experience the tour a second time at Wembley Stadium. It was large-scale group healing. Through her music, Taylor processed emotions en masse and created a sense of belonging you'd be hard-pressed to replicate. If you're a Swiftie reading this, you totally get the emotional high. If you're not, let me explain some of the science behind what you may perceive as glittering madness.

When people sing together, their heartbeats synchronise. Researchers from Gothenburg University monitored a choir and found their pulses sped up and slowed down at the same rate due to their breathing being coordinated. They also found singing had the overall effect of decreasing anxiety.[1] If you went to Taylor, you'd know this all too well.

When you bring your voiceprint to the fore and speak with authenticity, you join the choir of the world. No lip syncing allowed. Your voice carries its own frequency – a note only you can play. Sure, others may speak on the same topic, but nobody can speak about it in *your* way with *your* voice.

If you've ever felt there wasn't room for your voice – remember this: *not* using your voice is like ripping a piano key from the music of life.

The best thing you can do for world harmony is to use your voice. Not using it creates dissonance.

The crucial first step in the V.O.I.C.E
Formula is V for VIBRATIONS.

How do you strike your note?
It starts with breath. Remember, we pause on the 'in' breath and speak on the 'out' breath. The outgoing air travels from your lungs, up your windpipe and passes between your vocal cords (or folds), causing them to vibrate.

Try this: put your hand on your throat and *hummm*. Feel those buzzing vibrations? That's your vocal cords in action. Did your curiosity cause you to google 'vocal cords while singing' earlier? You would have seen that they look a lot like something else! For women, it's a reminder of our two great portals of expression. The word *cervix* actually means 'neck'. Fascinating, right?

Anyway, back to the top part of the body. As the air passes through your vocal cords, they vibrate. This sets off a chain reaction of vibrations in your body's resonance chambers, creating – *you guessed it* – resonance.

What is resonance?
Resonance is the quality and intensity of your vocal

tone. You'll hear the word *tone* used a lot more than resonance, but they're basically interchangeable. The word *resonance* comes from the Latin *resonantia*, meaning 'to resound'.

How would you describe your vocal tone?
Some of my clients complain about sounding too young, too old, too high-pitched, too squeaky, too nasal, too weak. The word 'too' is a giveaway they haven't settled into the true frequency of their voice. Through the lens of the anatomical voiceprint, this is usually due to an imbalance in the resonance chambers.

What are your resonance chambers?
1. Hollows of the head
Too much resonance up here makes the voice shrill and gets into that high pitch territory only dogs and small children can hear.

2. Nasal cavity
Too much resonance here creates an unpleasant nasal twang. It's often linked to a clenched jaw – more on that later.

3. Mouth

You can't avoid vibrations here when you speak, but if you *only* use this area, your voice will sound thin, weak and lacking any sort of gravitas.

4. Throat

Excessive resonance in the back of the throat produces a heavy, pompous tone. (If you're listening to the audiobook version of this, you'll hear me demonstrating the sounds as we go.)

5. Chest cavity

The only thing in your life you want to be down-and-out is your vocal vibrations! The best speakers know how to bring their vibrations down to the powerful heart space.

How do you find the core frequency of your voice?

Let's start at the beginning.

I was at another silent retreat. A nice weekend one – with reading, writing, as much as you could eat and a little chanting *cheat*. Yes, for one hour we sat in a room and chanted *"OM"* to our vocal cords' content.

"Something not a lot of people know," explained the

retreat leader Kara, who *could* talk, of course, "it's not actually *OM*."

My attention piqued.

"It's a three-syllable sound – *AUM*."

As someone who loves practising yoga and writes phonetic transcriptions for fun, this collision of interests exploded into a niche made for me.

As Kara described the three sounds, I was dying to blurt out: *"Yes. Yes. Yes. I totally get it. AUM starts with a diphthong, and OM starts with a pure vowel sound."* Let's face it, even if I could break the silence with this information, I would've broken any expectation that I was remotely cool. So, I just smiled to myself, before bathing in the vibrational beauty of 45 minutes of individual voices, including my own, creating a choir of *AUM*s.

It was raw. It was real. It felt primordial. And it is. Indian scriptures say *AUM* is the original sound from which all other sounds and creations emerged. It's widely believed it was the first sound emitted when the universe was created.[2]

***AUM* is the first sound you need to make to discover and embrace your own vocal vibrations.**

As I nerdily mentioned, *AUM* starts with a diphthong, which is a sound made by combining two vowel sounds in one syllable. Your mouth moves from one vowel shape to another – like in the word 'out' or 'loud'.

> **EXERCISE**
> *AUM*
>
> Chant *AUM* and pay attention to all three parts:
>
> Ah – jaw open, tongue down. Feel the vibrations in your chest.
> Oh (like in 'hot') – lips rounded. Focus the vibrations in your mouth.
> Mm – lips together, sound flowing out the nose.
> *Oh, it's so refreshing!*
>
> Really take your time on each of the sounds, especially the final *mmm* and enjoy the wonderful full body stretch for your voice.
>
> Keep going! The longer you chant, the more you'll attune to your soul frequency and the benefits will go beyond improving your voice.

Dr Herbert Benson pioneered research in the 1980s that shows repetition of a word or sound activates the parasympathetic nervous system, leading to a deep state of relaxation and reduced stress – remember the Las Vegas nerve?[3]

More recently, the Karolinska Institute in Sweden found that when we hum, we generate 15–20 times the usual number of nitric oxide molecules.[4] Nitric oxide improves blood flow and also has antifungal, antiviral and antibacterial qualities. So, if you feel yourself coming down with something, humming could help ward it off!

Why chant?

- Better concentration and focus
- Better immunity and self-healing power
- Opens the sinuses to clear the airways
- Puts you in a deep state of relaxation
- Better control over your emotions
- Decreases blood pressure
- Strengthens your spinal cord *and* vocal cords

> **EXERCISE**
> **Bumble Bee Breathing
> (Bhramari Pranayama)**
>
> This is like chanting, but without opening your mouth.
>
> Put your hand on your heart, take a breath low and deep into the body through the nose and "hummm" on the exhale.
>
> Feel yourself buzzing like the queen bumble bee you are!

Once you settle into your core frequency – your original sound – you can extend your vibrations throughout your vocal channel.

Let me explain: physiologically, our voice vibrates in the resonance chambers I described earlier. Energetically, it vibrates up and down the chakra *channel*. I believe this is a much easier way to visualise your voice and, in turn, change your sound.

For example, you might've heard you need to lower the pitch of your voice to be taken seriously, especially if you're a woman. This confusing advice can prompt you to push your voice to the back of your throat chamber, producing that pompous, fake sound that comes with excessive pharyngeal (throat) resonance. When your voice is hiding in the back of the body, you're energetically hiding your true self, which is why it sounds 'put on'.

Elizabeth Holmes adopted this kind of voice in her con job with startup Theranos. It's a rabbit hole worth diving into on a rainy day, but the short version is that Elizabeth Holmes is an American biotech entrepreneur who was convicted of fraud after she claimed her company revolutionised blood testing. She spoke in an unusually deep baritone voice during most of her public appearances. In a 2023 *New York Times* interview, Elizabeth spoke in her natural, higher-pitched voice and confirmed the low voice was a facade.[5]

Don't get me wrong, there is incredible value in lowering the pitch of your voice for certain scenarios – as long as you know how to do it authentically.

Forget pitch, focus on position.
It's less about lowering your voice and more about expanding your vocal range. It's about having greater

access to parts of the vocal channel that best match the meaning of what you're saying. That's the definition of speaking in alignment.

Let's explore three key vibration areas along your vocal channel: your head, your heart and your solar plexus (upper abdomen).

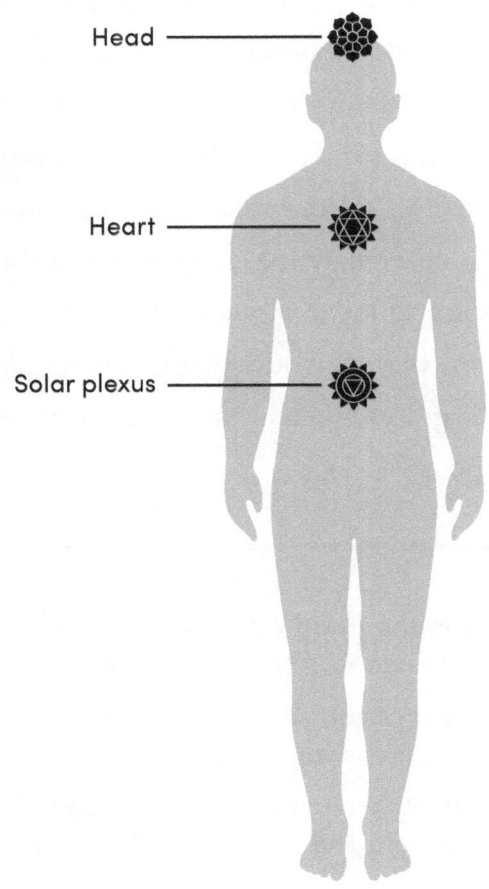

1. Vibrations in Your Head

Key chakra – crown
Key resonance chambers – hollows of the head and nasal cavity

Take a breath in. On the exhale, visualise the sound coming out the top of your head as you say "eeeee." If you place your hands over your eyes and nasal cavity, you should be able to feel those vibrations coming through your skull. If you can't, try for a bit more volume.

I hear many voices stuck up in this area. Overthinking, overanalysing, and overstressing can cause your voice to lodge in your head, disconnecting it from the rest of your body. If this sounds like you, go back to the grounding and breathing exercises from previous chapters.

> **Vibrate in the head when you want your audience to THINK something.**
>
> *Like those original concepts and ideas you introduce.*
>
> Example: "If strangers see your voice as a goldmine, imagine what it's worth to you."

2. Vibrations in Your Heart
Key chakra – heart
Key resonance chamber – upper chest cavity

Let's move down to your chest – your beautiful heart chakra space, the energy centre of love and compassion. Put your left hand on your chest, take a deep breath into your hand, and on the exhale, say "haaaaa." Feel the vibrations on the palm of your hand? Do you notice a sense of calm or being more centred?

> **Vibrate in the heart space when you want your audience to FEEL something.**
>
> *Like those emotional stories and examples you share.*
>
> Example: "I realised my life's mission was to help people find their inner fire and channel it through their soul-stirring voice."

3. Vibrations in Your Solar Plexus

Key chakra – solar plexus
Key resonance chamber – lower chest cavity

Finally, let's focus on the solar plexus, located in your upper belly, right where your diaphragm runs. This is the seat of your self-belief and self-esteem. Take a deep breath, then imagine you're speaking from the solar plexus as you say "yeh yeh yeh." (If you're Australian and over 40, this might remind you of the tagline for Advanced Hair: "Yeah yeah!") Notice how the sound emanates from the middle of your body?

> **Vibrate in the solar plexus when you want your audience to DO something.**
>
> *Like those practical calls to action you make.*
>
> Example: "Do a voice warm-up every day in the shower."

Think of a speaker you admire. Chances are, they instinctively use all three of these resonance spaces. You can learn to as well.

> ## **EXERCISE**
> ### Counting
>
> This exercise is fantastic to practise accessing each of those three areas along the vocal channel – head, heart and solar plexus.
>
> - Visualise the numbers 1–10 as big 3D models around the room. Some on the floor, some on the ceiling, in all the corners too!
>
> - Using your hand, physically pull the numbers towards you as you count from 1 to 10.
>
> - Vary speaking from your head, heart and solar plexus. Let your hand finish at the part of your body you're using to speak each number.

How did that feel? Did you know your voice could do that? Like learning a new musical instrument, it takes practice. The dedication is worth it. When your vocal vibrations are aligned with your intentions, the message lands authentically. This transcends the sound waves that leave your mouth and land on the ears of your listener.

PART TWO

Your vibrations resonate beyond the physical body.

Have people or places given you good or bad vibes? You might call it your spidey sense or your intuition. Think of it like an antenna. We are human radio stations constantly sending and receiving frequencies. Imagine that the little wi-fi icon sits above your head. You can't see it; you can't hear it; you can't touch it — but everyone knows whether or not it's working! How strong is the signal you're sending when you speak?

It's important to set the energy, not *get* the energy as a speaker.

Of course, the audience *can* fuel your energy, but you shouldn't rely on it. I was once tasked with delivering company-wide training in the manufacturing industry to help team leaders deliver more effective toolbox talks. Executives didn't want anyone to miss this important training, but you could only imagine the reception I received from the night shift team, who stared down the barrel of a 4-hour workshop at 6 am!

I needed to turn the understandable groans into grins, and energetically reset the mood.

> **Your energy speaks louder than your words.**

You want your vibration to be the signal the whole room connects into.

As a reiki practitioner, I've seen firsthand the power of harnessing vibrations we can't see – specifically with clearing voice blocks. Reiki translates to *universal energy*, of which there is an abundance. Many of those unseen forces were at play at Taylor Swift's Eras Tour!

The week before the concert, I was in California experiencing my voice like never before. I'd heard about this place called the Reality Center in a fascinating documentary on Gaia, which is basically Netflix for spiritual people. *Self-healing through your own voice!?* That was all the motivation I needed to jump on a plane to LA.

In a dark room, I lay back in what resembled a dentist's chair, but instead of drills, the vibrations were coming from my own voice. As I waxed lyrical about my perfect day and the things that bring me joy and peace, a rainbow of chakra-coloured bars danced in a graph on the screen in front of me. It was breaking my voice down to its essence, capturing a snapshot of my unique vibration.

Then came the magic: using that personalised data, they played specific frequencies *back* to me. This is called biofeedback – literally getting a dose of your own vocal medicine. Like being hooked up to a voice IV drip, I walked out completely recharged, laser-focused, and more connected to my purpose than ever. In fact, the first stirrings of this book took shape right there in that chair.

It was a divine experience and proves we're only scratching the surface of the healing potential of our voice. The most mind-blowing part was watching the vibrational data shift right before my eyes as I changed the *intention* behind my words.

**It's not just what you say;
it's the energy you bring.**

When you speak from your head, heart, and solar plexus, aligned and attuned, you're broadcasting a frequency uniquely yours. That's what chanting *AUM* unlocks.

That's what Taylor tapped into. And that's what makes your voiceprint truly resonate.

> **YOUR VIBRATIONS AFFIRMATION**
> "I have the power to bring the good vibes."

"Open yourself and flow, my friend. Flow in the total openness of the living moment."

BRUCE LEE

CHAPTER 9
O = OPENNESS

"So, there I was. Lying in the fetal position on the couch rocking my bottle of merlot."

Many a good story of mine includes this line. A nod to my binging, boozing, bacchanalian past. A representation of constriction and closing. A manifestation of fear and shame. The fetal position is a biological regression to safety, to the womb, to the only place our nervous system once knew complete protection. This is why when fear creeps in, your shoulders hunch. When you doubt yourself, your solar plexus collapses. When you're afraid to speak your truth, your chin snaps down like a gate.

> Your beautiful voice can only flow if
> the channel is open to allow it.

PART TWO

That's why the O in our V.O.I.C.E Formula is for OPENNESS.

- If we **close our minds**, we limit our potential.
- If we **close our bodies**, we restrict our expression.
- If we **close our mouths**, we silence our truth.

Without opening – mentally, physically and vocally – our voiceprint cannot fully emerge. Opening up can feel daunting. It means being exposed, being vulnerable, being seen, and perhaps most terrifying of all – being judged. And nothing shuts you down faster than a fear of those things.

"I'm going to make TikToks."

It was late 2019, and the fellow businesswomen I told nodded with encouragement, though their confusion was hard to hide.

Back then, it was a singing, dancing app for kids. No place for a 30-something-year-old coach to clock up credibility. The ill-founded reputation of TikTok gave me an incredible sense of comfort. I could be as bra-free open as I wanted because, hey, hardly anyone I knew was on there.

In the beginning, I followed the music and lip-syncing trends. But it wasn't until I spoke straight down the barrel of the camera – confident, clear and so keen I forgot to brush my lashes (which the good people of TikTok were quick to point out) – that I broke through.

"*Babe*, something's happened!"

Poor Patrick was on a military exercise interstate and thought there was an actual emergency.

"Have you seen my TikTok?!"

Patrick was my first follower.

"Like, 60,000 people have seen it."

They talk about your phone blowing up. I get it. I was torn between being glued to the rising views and throwing the whole device out the window. I couldn't refresh fast enough to keep up, and replying to every comment had me wishing I'd taken thumb wars more seriously in primary school. Talk about commenter's cramp! I went from 45 followers to more than 10,000 in less than 7 days – and it kept growing and growing and growing. That video has racked up almost 2 million views at last look. Many of my subsequent TikToks

PART TWO

followed suit. What a time to be alive!

It's easy to be bold and open when everyone loves you. But just like a stronger magnet pulls in more metallic trash, and a brighter sun reaches people who want to stay in the dark, inevitably reaching a bigger audience opens you up to the slings and arrows of the masses.

Here's a taste of my comments section:

> *Your voice is so annoying. Shut up.*

> *Covid has really given the 'special' people something to get their 15 seconds of flop. Hasn't it?*

> *You're so god damn annoying. It's worth my time to tell you how annoying you are. It's therapeutic. PS Nobody cares.*

> *No offence but I switch off when you speak.*

> *Lady you really need some good hard D. Who do you think you are with your condescending tone.*

> *I cannot stand Australian middle aged women who talk like this.*

> *Her hair, face, voice and everything irritates me.*

I mean, pretty hilarious – and I used to have a series called 'Hate Comments Read Like a Newsreader', so the material was welcome.

In one video, someone photoshopped the poo emoji onto my head and called me Australia's most condescending woman. I commented that it was apt as I used to be a spokesperson for a sewerage company. He replied asking what 'apt' meant. I didn't want to explain it for fear of sounding condescending.

Only a couple of social media videos and comments really cut deep. The ones that criticised the core of who I am and what I stand for.

In early 2022, I posted a TikTok about pronunciation. I was coaching a lot of TV news reporters at the time who dutifully wanted to correctly pronounce key words in their stories – and I thought it would make for an innocent, helpful talking point on social media.

Well, people were keyboard-ready.

> *Yeh, I've always had bad vibes about that lady.*

> *Don't let this woman tell you how to speak.*

> *She's dangerous.*

PART TWO

The comments were in direct contravention to the reason I do this work and create content. So, there I was – lying in the fetal position on my coach's couch rocking my bottle of merlot.

"Why are they so mean?! They don't know me!"

"Sal, listen to me," she handed me a tissue. "You gotta live life in your disco ball. Keep on shining, keep on dancing. You decide who comes to your party, and the rest are looking at their own reflection."

She followed that up by this banger – "Anyone pointing a judgey finger has three pointing right back on themselves."

That coaching session marked a major turning point. I swapped the merlot on the couch for melting heart pose on the yoga mat and gave significantly fewer fucks about online criticism.

Granted, I also have a background as a TV journalist where the horrible hustle is real. Getting hung up on, having doors slammed in your face, being flipped the bird, even spat on outside the local courthouse were not unusual before the afternoon deadline. And just when you thought you'd survived the day, your boss would berate you for your make-up skills: "Haven't you heard of an eyebrow pencil?" You just got on with it. To be fair, my facial hair *is* fair.

"If it's that bad, why don't you quit?" Mum asked a valid question after I vented about a particularly hard day. *Why didn't I?* It's not like the meagre salary had me in golden handcuffs. It was because the excitement and satisfaction of meeting people and telling their stories far outweighed the negative. The good outshone the bad.

> **The light of being open always beats the darkness of closing up.**

Sure, when you open yourself, you open up to criticism and judgement, rejection and failure. I've seen it play out. The critics are poised like vultures, hoping you'll retreat behind a door. Closing up is a coping mechanism and – let's be honest – the easy option. Don't give them that satisfaction. Reframe that damn door.

Showing up online or speaking on stage is not putting yourself in danger; it's a chance to open your heart to love, joy and support. Many thriving online communities are built on the backs of courageous creators who took the risk to open up and share their truth.

All these years later, I'm still proudly posting on social media. I'm not afraid of criticism. In fact, I welcome it. It might bring another breakthrough.

Such is the freedom of operating with an open mind and open heart.

This sets the scene for an open vocal channel.

Do you wish you were better at speaking off the cuff or thinking on your feet? All you need to do is open your energetic channel, right up to the crown chakra, and let the direct downloads flow in. If you've ever expressed yourself with surprising eloquence then forgotten what you just said – that's a sign the divine was moving through you.

Remember the antenna from the last chapter? We're like little TVs, and God, Source, the Universe (whatever you like to call it) is the transmission tower. If we're blocked with negative thoughts and doubts and a crappy speaking story, the signal gets interrupted, and we end up with glitchy, fuzzy reception. If we open our channel, we're clear to receive the signal through our crown, and it flows out via our voice.

> **Your body needs to reflect this openness before you even start speaking.**

That means:
- **Open your stance** so the audience feels on solid ground with you as a speaker. As a high-heel wearer, I understand the urge to do the whole legs-crossed weight-shifting dance. Toughen up or wear flats. The audience doesn't want to sense your discomfort or wonder if you need to do a wee.
- **Open your shoulders** so your heart chakra shines and your breath flows easily. Have you ever seen a confident speaker closed and hunched? No, their posture is open and inviting. Unravel yourself from the comfort-fetal position and put on your angel wings. This is an excellent visual to help keep your shoulders back.
- **Open your palms** so your gestures are warm and inviting. Dictators do a lot of palm-down pointing. Real leaders hold their audience gently in the palm of their hand.
- **Open your throat** so your voice is free to flow. Keep your eyes up. Where the eyes go, the chin

will follow. If the chin points down, it kinks your air supply like a tangled garden hose.
- **Open your jaw** so your voice can be heard and understood. I realise 'open your mouth' may not read as groundbreaking speaking advice, but a tight jaw is the most common cause of mumbling and poor projection.

A closed jaw is the great Australian blight – I'm surprised we haven't produced more famous ventriloquists. Have you heard the reason we don't open our jaws here in Australia?

Yes, it's so the blowflies don't get in! If you've visited the outback, you'll see they have a point. But unless you're presenting your speech outdoors in summer, it's literally a joke of an excuse.

Try slowly opening your jaw now. If you're reading this in public, just ignore the strange looks. Now massage your jaw gently at that hinge where your lower jaw connects to your skull. Little circles with your fingertips one way, then the other. Now, slowly drag your hands down the sides of your face to release tension, and open your mouth, like you're screaming in a silent movie.

I have more jaw-dropping exercises later in the book.

My favourite exercise for opening your body – including your stance, shoulders, palms, throat and jaw – is one I call Butterfly Breathing.

EXERCISE
Butterfly Breathing

- Stand with your legs hip-width apart.

- Ensure your head is up and your jaw is open as you breathe in while spreading your arms out wide like butterfly wings. Everything is wide open.

- As you breathe out, bring your arms in and wrap them around your body, giving yourself a big hug. Your mouth closes, and your chin tilts down.

- Then repeat. Breathe in and open. Breathe out and close.

This exercise will also improve your everyday posture, something I've been quite blessed with.

"You have amazing posture, Sal." I hear this compliment frequently.

It could be all the experience speaking on stage. It could be all the yoga. Or it could be my high school friend Sonia – the same one who rang me post-Vipassana – always telling me to make the 'breast' of things.

"Chin up, chest out," she'd say. It was excellent advice. "Open your heart chakra," might have sounded less gauche, but "chin up, chest out" is way more memorable. It's all in the alliteration, juxtaposition, and cheekiness of the phrase. Sonia has a hell of a voiceprint – and I still hear her saying that line in my head before stepping on stage.

**What will remind you to be more open
in the way you use your voice?**

I wrote a little poem you could borrow:

Not sure where to start?
Open your mind and your heart.
The critics are here to stay,
so open yourself anyway.
If you feel the urge to doubt,
remember my friend – chin up, chest out.
Butterfly breathe, wear your wings

and enjoy the feeling being open brings.
Next time you rise to speak,
let your voiceprint be strong, not weak.
With your energetic channel open and ready to go,
your beautiful voice will flow, flow, flow.

> **YOUR OPENNESS AFFIRMATION**
> "I am open and ready to receive."

"It's not what I say, but the way I say it."

MAE WEST

CHAPTER 10
I = INTONATION

"*Canta,* Sally, *canta*!"

I'd been living in Brazil for less than 3 months, and my Portuguese was gringa-central, meaning I was struggling!

"*Eu. Es-tou. Ten-tan-do.*" I'm Trying!

"*Canta,* Sally, *canta.*" Sing, Sally, sing.

Brazilian Portuguese has a beautiful musicality to it. It's the accent, the *sotaque,* and the *intonation* that makes the language sound like a song. It's one of the main characteristics that separates it from the Portuguese of Portugal, which sounds a bit more staccato – short and choppy. When I think of English dialects with a singsongy musical quality, the ones that come to mind are the Irish and Welsh accents. What comes to mind for you?

PART TWO

No matter what language you speak or accent you use, intonation gives your speech colour and rich emotional meaning.

Without it we'd sound like those early text-to-speech electronics. You'd intellectually process the words, but at best you'd lose the emotional connection and at worst completely misinterpret the meaning. This is why learning a language is about so much more than memorising vocabulary. As I discovered in those early months in Brazil, saying the words without the matching intonation meant people usually had no idea *what* I was saying. I wish Duolingo existed back then!

Whether English is your native language or not, chances are you need to brush up on how to use intonation. I know this, because whenever I do classes on this topic for my Soul Speakers community, people's minds are blown and voices are changed for the better. Think of a speaker you find particularly captivating. I'd bet my voiceprint it's their use of intonation drawing you in.

That's why the I in our V.O.I.C.E Formula is for INTONATION.

What is intonation?

In the context of speaking, intonation is the rise and fall of the voice.

Try it out aloud now:

My voice can rise.

My voice can fall.

See how it adds musicality to your speech?

What's the difference between pitch and intonation?

Pitch is like an elevator or lift – it's the vertical ups and downs. Your voice box physically moves up and down in your throat as you produce different pitches (you can feel it.) More on this when we get to the Expression chapter.

Intonation is more like a skate ramp – it's the *movement* of the pitch as it rises and falls. These movements are called inflections. Pitch is hitting the singular piano key; intonation is sliding up and down all the keys. Pitch is static; intonation is fluid.

If you're reading this thinking, *Bloody hell, I didn't sign up for something quite so technical*, let me tell you a secret. If you can use intonation correctly and creatively when you speak, I promise you people will turn and listen – and have no idea why.

PART TWO

> I call it the Intonation Advantage – few
> have it, but those who do own the room.

You're stepping into an elite group here. I'm teaching you the secret handshake of the most compelling speakers, programming the codes of your voiceprint that unlock a VIP pass to influence. Are you ready for your intonation lesson? Class is in session.

Intonation 101 – the two golden rules:
1. Rise when you're not finished speaking
2. Fall when you are

The rising inflection is like the comma of punctuation, while the falling inflection is like the full stop. When you're *not* done speaking, you need to cue the audience to keep listening, while you take a pause, and that's why you use the rising inflection. It's like a song where the chord progression isn't resolved, or a TV show that ends on a cliff hanger; you keep people on the hook – until you're ready to grant sweet release.

To execute this well, gradient matters. An extremely sharp rising inflection that shoots up like the Tower of Terror generally won't sound good. Likewise, a falling inflection that plummets off the side of a mountain will also sound weird. Think of the rise as a dolphin gracefully surfacing from the water and the fall as more of an outward motion, like throwing a dart.

I call this the Target Technique.
At the end of your phrase, imagine you're throwing the last stressed word or syllable like a dart soaring into the bullseye of a dartboard.

So instead of this.
You get this.

EXERCISE
Target Technique Practice

- Scrunch up some scrap paper.
- Say the following sentences aloud into a mirror, and as you say the part bolded and underlined, throw the paper at the mirror.
    - Thanks for being here to**night**.
    - It's such an important point to **make**.
    - My name is (insert your name and relevant emphasis) Sally **Pros**ser.

If you break golden rule one and rise when you *are* finished speaking, you get:

The Inflection of Validation

This is when the voice goes up ↗ ... at the end of every line ↗ ... even when it's a complete statement ↗ ... like this ↗ ... You may have heard it referred to as uptalk or HRT (high rising terminal). It's quite common in New Zealand, Australia and California (think valley girl, surfer dude – "*Like, totally*"). This speech pattern is **not inherently a bad thing.** Remember the chameleon effect I mentioned earlier in the book? Uptalk likely developed as a way to reinforce social bonding. [6]

There's a great comedy skit by Adam Hills where he says, "You know what we do here in Australia? I'm sure you're aware we all go up at the end of every sentence. 'Cause we're all too insecure to make a statement, so we have to make it sound like a question ... Susie got eaten by a *shark*?"[7] Adam is comically correct. Going up at the end of a complete statement is plagued with voiceprint problems.

But hang on, aren't you supposed to go up when you ask a question?

Yes, yes you are. But it's not *all* questions, only questions that can be answered by *yes* or *no*. These are closed questions like: Are you enjoying this book? Do you know what I mean? When you use the rising inflection on a *complete statement,* you're unconsciously seeking yes/no validation from your listener. You're unsure of what you're saying, so you plead for reassurance. You're asking the audience to give you the big thumbs up or thumbs down like you're a defeated gladiator in the Colosseum putting the fate of your life in the mood of the masses.

This *pollice verso* is undertaken by your modern-day spectators: people on the other side of the interview room or meeting table or news camera or social media lens. When the listener hears complete statements delivered like Y/N questions – such as, "I have twenty years' experience," "The team is taking action" – they aren't thinking *Oh, your intonation's off,* they're receiving subconscious cues that you're not believable, not trustworthy, and probably not cut out for the job. Chances are you deserve none of those assumptions. But your voiceprint speaks louder than any words on paper.

PART TWO

Your intonation overrides the words you say.

Read that again. The most articulate, impressive words will lose effect if delivered with dodgy intonation.

Why do you do this unhelpful 'going up' thing with your voice?

It goes back to Part One: if you're spinning a record of doubt, apprehension and second-guessing in your head, this is one of the ways it comes out in your physical voice. The inner impostor and judge and critic and perfectionist and people pleaser love to hijack your intonation and sabotage your speaking success.

What can you do about it?

Stop searching for validation externally. Wrangle that chariot of inner voices to work for your highest intention and practise the Target Technique.

Now, if you break the golden rule two of intonation and fall when you're *not* finished speaking, then you get:

The Inflection of Deflation

This is the opposite of keeping people's attention on the hook. In fact↘. Every line↘. Goes down↘. Like this↘. And it's a struggle to keep your eyes open, let alone hear the message!

When I was a kid, I loved playing a computer game called *Lemmings*, where hundreds of human-like lemmings with green hair and blue robes would walk out into different lands in a perfect single-file line. You, as the controller, had to find ways to redirect them to safety; otherwise they marched right off a cliff. A steady stream of lemmings falling to their demise. That is what the Inflection of Deflation reminds me of – poor little phrases falling to their deaths, one after the other after the other.

Forget Death by PowerPoint, this is death by inflection point.

You'll relate if you've ever heard a leader open a meeting and use the Inflection of Deflation as they say: "Good morning↘. Good to be here↘." It's about as inspiring as a soggy rice cake.

How can you avoid this bus to boredom?

Rise and shine! Visualise that each of your phrases has

a small upward arrow at the end, a dot-dot-dot ... a compelling comma. In your mind's eye, see the dolphin rise up out of the water, and use gestures. Raising your arm will help raise your voice and keep your audience on the edge of their seat, until you're ready to – remember – grant sweet release!

Okay, great work, class.

Once you get the basics of rising when you're *not* finished speaking and falling when you *are* (Target Technique), then you can layer-up with some fancy intonation magic.

I'll share three of my favourites:

1. The Tease and Land

Forget the Bend and Snap, meet the Tease and Land.

It's a rising inflection, followed by a pause, followed by the Target Technique. And it sounds .|. like this.

This technique:
- Reels the audience in ↗
- Holds their attention |
- Drops your point with impact ◉

I also call this the Mic-Drop Moment because that's what this technique achieves – a hushed response of *drop the damn mic.*

First, find a phrase in your speech that's a real mic-drop moment – a quotable quote, a line someone in the audience would type in a LinkedIn post about the talk. Phrases that have a question-and-answer style work perfectly. Place a line like this │ where you'd take the pause, an upward arrow on the stressed syllable before the pause, and an underline or target on the stressed syllable after it.

For example:
- If you have your brea↗th │ you have your vo⊙ice.
- It's not *what* you sa↗y │ it's the energy you br⊙ing.
- I needed to go qui↗et │ to continue being he⊙ard.

Now that you're aware of this technique, you'll hear it everywhere. Professional speakers use it all the time, and you're probably already doing it subconsciously, especially when you feel confident.

The word 'confidence' comes from the Latin *confidere*, meaning 'to trust'. And that's the key. **It takes trust in yourself to pause.** I challenge you to hold the pause just a little longer ... than what feels comfortable.

Nailing the Tease and Land shows ultimate confidence and will have your audience whispering *wow*.

2. The Inflection of Suggestion

This is when you rise at the end of a phrase, even if you *are* finished, and pair it with a subtle head nod or shake. This signals to the listener to answer the question with the yes/no answer *you suggest*.

For example:

- "*Voiceprint* is an incredible read." With a rising inflection and a head nod, the audience agrees.
- "No one wants to have a mental block while speaking." With a rising inflection and a head shake, the audience agrees.

See how you can plant the suggestion?

Sometimes you are genuinely *wanting* feedback from your audience, so you can also use this speech pattern to garner a response. You're opening up the floor by framing a statement as a question. For example: "We're planning to roll this out across the business." You'll soon find out what people think of this plan!

The Inflection of Suggestion is a powerful technique for leaders to assert themselves in the spirit of collaboration, because the tone is inviting, not demanding.

3. The Lulling Effect

"That's right. Can those eyes just stay closed as you're comfort ... able to go deeper, just like ... when ... you ... go ... to sleep."

My eyelids felt like lead curtains. I couldn't keep them open, and my feet were glued to the floor. The instructor's voice was in my veins.

"Have you noticed your hands lifting, lifting, lifting even more lightly, even more easily?" My hands took on a life of their own and began moving up in front of my face. I thought I was controlling it. Was I?

During my hypnosis practitioner training, we spent hours in trance. It was deeply relaxing, quite trippy and very funny. We may have witnessed a wedding to a fictional donkey serenaded by a global superstar. If you've ever been under hypnosis, you know the sensation well.

When you're in trance, the brain transitions from beta waves (active thinking) to alpha waves (relaxed focus) and even theta waves (deep relaxation, dream-like state). Theta waves are powerful for learning, healing and behaviour change because we have increased suggestibility, creativity and memory access. Basically, we're more adaptable and easier to rewire.[8]

So, if you're wanting to teach, heal, change behaviour, shift beliefs or introduce a new way of thinking – getting the audience into trance is a very effective tool. As speakers we usually want to facilitate some kind of transformation.

Voice, particularly strategic intonation, plays a crucial role in inducing trance states. Keep the phrases rhythmic, moving up and down like you're wandering over rolling hills, rising and falling, rising and falling, reducing your pauses and rising and falling, leaning on key words as you travel.

For example, in one of my talks, I use the Lulling Effect when I say, "And as you sit here listening to these words … you might begin to notice … just how powerful your own voice can be."

If an audience is in the palm of your hand, totally captivated, almost open-mouthed and drooling – that's a sign you may have induced a trance state.

Now, unless you're a stage hypnotist wanting everyone to cluck like chickens, I recommend scattering the Lulling Effect carefully throughout your speech – certainly don't use it on every phrase!

It's pretty incredible, isn't it? Controlling the ebb and flow of intonation when you speak is like being handed a baton to conduct your audience.

One caveat to keep in mind with intonation: language is always evolving, and context is everything. As mentioned at the start of the chapter, this is also where accents play a major role. The speech patterns that affect perceptions today may not be the same ones future researchers uncover. But when you have the Intonation Advantage, you'll be ready for anything, because your voiceprint holds the codes.

From here, pay attention to the rise and fall of your voice, experiment with these techniques and watch how people lean in. Master your intonation, and you'll master the room.

Class dismissed.

YOUR INTONATION AFFIRMATION
"I trust in the musical flow of my voice."

"You are a human being with a soul and the divine gift of articulate speech ... don't sit there crooning like a bilious pigeon."

GEORGE BERNARD SHAW

CHAPTER 11
C = CLARITY

"What brings you here this afternoon?"

I was standing at a bar on a Saturday evening, and striking up a flirty conversation with an attractive stranger vaguely in my age bracket seemed like the thing to do.

He looked quite taken aback, "Oh, my mate's just been cremated."

"Oh, gosh, I'm *so* sorry to hear that. Are you okay?" I've been around death more than I'd like, so I'm not scared to lean into these kinds of conversations.

"Yeah, we were all expecting it." He seemed numb.

"Oh, I imagine that makes it a little easier." I feared he was shutting his emotions down. I was the woman to bring them out.

"He's here with us." I gestured to my heart.

"Yes, he is here with us." He nodded in fierce agreement.

Oh yes, spiritual king. My checklist got a tick.

"I believe when our loved ones are Earthside, they're somewhere, and when they leave, they're everywhere," I said wistfully and starry-eyed.

He gave me the *who is this crazy lady?* look and cautiously backed away. "Um, I've gotta get these drinks back, he's waiting right over there."

"Sorry, what?"

It. All. Starts. To. Dawn.

"Oooooh! Your mate hasn't been *cremated*, he's been *promoted!*"

The 'crazy lady' look lingered as he scurried off.

I smiled. A champagne and a brilliant anecdote. More than you get from most bar chats.

> **Articulation matters. There is power in precise speech. That's why the C in our V.O.I.C.E Formula stands for CLARITY.**

We all have a hilarious lost-in-translation story – often relating to cross-cultural communication.

Laetitia, my client I mentioned in Part One with

the breathing, runs new moon circles. One circle, we were urged over and over to release our inner walrus. I was straining my brain and googling the spirit animal meaning of the *walrus*, feeling a bit confused. Finally, it came up in the chat, and Laetitia clarified in her beautiful French accent that she was actually urging us to release our inner *warrioress*.

Patrick, as a health and safety manager, was alarmed to hear there were pits appearing on every level of the office. What a major hazard! His colleague has a broad Kiwi accent, and Patrick was relieved to discover there were in fact *pets* on every level, not giant holes in the floor.

And there are many stories I could regale you with from my time in Brazil. One of the trickier words to pronounce is *pão*, meaning bread, as the ã is produced through the nose. *Pau*, the same word but produced through the mouth, is slang for the male sex organ. Let's just say, I went into the supermarket one day thinking I was asking for Turkish bread but loudly ordered Turkish something else.

Most of the time, these misunderstandings do no harm and make fodder for funny stories. But if you have an important message to convey, clarity of speech is no laughing matter. Sometimes it's a question of life and death. A misheard word has been to blame in countless aviation disasters and failed military operations.

One devastating example is Vera Mol, a Dutch teenager who was killed in a bungee jumping accident in Spain in 2015. She leapt from a bridge without her harness being fastened and fell more than 30 metres to her death, all because she heard "now jump" instead of "no jump."[9]

The stakes may not be so high in your speaking scenarios, but what if they *were*?

Whether you're heading up an emergency management team, delivering a client pitch or speaking to someone on the phone, clarity counts. Because here's the hard truth: you can have gorgeous vocal tone, be open and use on-point intonation, but if your words aren't clear, your message is fuzzy. If you stumble, tumble and bumble over your words, your message is diluted. And if people can't understand you at all, your message is entirely lost.

> **Sloppy speech is a real credibility killer.**

And I need to point out, if English isn't your native language, this isn't about accent reduction; it's about clarity production. Your accent is part of who you are, and we do not want to reduce you!

How do you speak with clarity?

Get to the speech gym and train your organs of speech!

Your organs of speech (or organs of articulation) are the body parts you use to form words:

- Jaw
- Lips
- Tongue
- Soft palate
- Hard palate
- Teeth

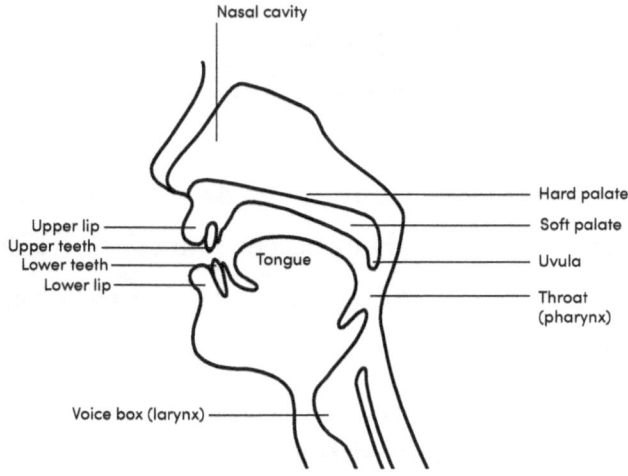

You can't move your hard palate or teeth, so we won't worry about those, though it's worth noting they do affect your speech. Anyone who's had braces or wears a retainer knows this firsthand.

Let's focus on your moveable organs of speech. Just like physical exercise, speech training has two parts:

1. Dedicated sessions to strengthen and tone
2. Warm-ups before speaking – like stretching before a race

Open your jaw

The number one thing you can do to improve your voiceprint, particularly clarity of speech, is to *open your mouth*. Be brave, risk the blowflies! A tight, closed jaw is the main reason for mumbling and also contributes to a nasal tone – the air isn't given the space to emerge from your mouth, so it pushes out your nose. When you present to an audience, you need to open your jaw wider than feels comfortable in your regular day to day.

In the Openness chapter, I promised more jaw exercises, and here they are.

Exercises for the Jaw

- **Massage:** take two fingers and make little circles where your lower jaw hinges to your skull.

- **The Surprised Donkey:** stretching your lips as much as you can, say *"ee-aw-ah."*

- **Bite your vowels:** say each of the vowels as though you're taking a bite out of an apple – A, E, I, O, U.

Relax your lips

If your lips are dry and tense, you'll struggle to open your jaw, and your tone will sound harsh. Think of a stereotypical office worker who has no sense of humour asking: "Where are those invoices?" Chances are it's delivered with a tight lip. Many nervous speakers trying to 'keep it together' will automatically tense their lips. No surprise, the phrase 'stiff upper lip' is associated with exercising emotional restraint.

Your lips come together for the sounds 'p', 'b' and 'm', and your upper teeth rest against your lower lip for 'f' and 'v'. You're on the road to Stumble Town on these sounds if you don't learn to relax your lips.

These are exercises you don't want to pay lip service to!

Exercises for the Lips

- **The Braying Horse:** sigh out and bray your lips – "brrrrr."
- **Boxing:** do a boxing action with your hands as you say "pah-pah-pah-*punch!*"
- **Eminem Challenge:** how many times can you say "Eminem" before messing it up?

Tone your tongue

The tongue is the strongest muscle in the body. Actually, that's a myth! On strength-to-size ratio, the masseter (jaw muscle) can exert the most force for its size, but the tongue *is* an incredibly important muscle for speaking, and the stronger it is, the clearer your speech will be.

Here's a random fact you'll never need: most of the consonant sounds come in cute little pairs – one voiced, one voiceless. For example: 't' and 'd', 's' and 'z', 'k' and 'g'. If you place your hand on your throat as you say them, you'll feel your vocal cords vibrate only on the second sound – 'd', 'z' and 'g'.

When the tongue is lazy, the voiced sound often replaces the voiceless one. That's why you'll hear 'rider' and not know whether they were on a horse or authoring a book. Of course, context usually clears it up! But, if you're looking to polish up your speech, enunciating your t's is a great place to start. I especially recommend popping your t's on the end of words when speaking to a large audience or outdoors – like in the word 'tonight'.

> ### Exercises for the Tongue
>
> - **French Exclamation:** say "oo-la-*la*" five times as fast as possible.
> - **Drum Kit:** like you're a beat boxer, repeat "d-t-t, d-t-t, d-t-t."
> - **Counting:** count from 20 to 40, making sure you enunciate every 't'. For example, it's twen<u>t</u>y-eigh<u>t</u> not twenny-aye.

Strengthen your soft palate

Your soft palate is connected to your hard palate. It's the soft squishy thing at the back of the roof of your mouth. The soft palate is attached to the uvula, which is the little dangly thing you see at the back of the throat when cartoon characters scream. It snaps with the back of your tongue to make the sounds 'k' and 'g', and closes and stays in place for 'm', 'n' and 'ng'. 'M', 'n' and 'ng' are what we call nasal sounds because the soft palate is blocking the airflow through the mouth like a trapdoor, forcing it to escape through the nose.

A lazy soft palate hangs down permanently, meaning *all* the sounds go through the nose, producing that annoying nasal twang. Pair that with a tight lower jaw and you are straight onto the set of Australian comedy *Kath & Kim*.

Exercises for the Soft Palate

- **Pac-Man:** say "ung-ung-ung" while imagining you're travelling along eating Pac-Man dots like in the arcade game.
- **Glug a drink:** say it and mimic the sound of glugging – "glug, glug, glug."
- **Yawn:** a nice big yawn lifts the soft palate creating open space at the back of the throat.

Hopefully you're not yawning in boredom, and these exercises have awakened clarity of both mind and speech! These are the types of warm-ups and exercises professional speakers do.

If you sat at the news desk, you'd likely be surprised how fast the autocue moves. News presenters make it sound easy because their speech fitness is so high. Even Ron Burgundy shows how it's done! "A tarantula enjoys a fine chewing gum" is my favourite *Anchorman* warm-up. Same goes for sports commentators, race callers and auctioneers – wow, speaking that fast *and* adding numbers so accurately is a special skill for sure!

Want to speak like the pros? I have three bonus tips:

1. Recite Shakespeare

If you can wrap your tongue around Shakespeare, you can wrap your tongue around anything. Now get your mind out of the gutter and into this apt monologue from *Hamlet* (act three, scene two):

> *Speak the speech, I pray you, as I pronounced it to you, trippingly on the tongue. But if you mouth it, as many of your players do, I had as lief the town-crier spoke my lines. Nor do not saw the air too much with your hand, thus, but use all gently; for in the very torrent, tempest, And, as I may say, the whirlwind of your passion, you must acquire and beget a temperance that may give it smoothness.*

If you can handle Shakespeare, everyday speech will be a breeze. It's like using paddles in swim training – those flat, plastic things you wear on your hands. When you take them off, your hands glide through the water as if it were air. Train with resistance so you can perform with graceful strength.

2. Have a tongue twister party trick

What's your favourite tongue twister? Mine is Betty Botter, who even has her own Wikipedia page!

> *Betty Botter bought some butter,*
> *but she said this butter's bitter.*
> *If I put it in my batter, it will make my batter bitter,*
> *but a bit of better butter will make my batter better.*
> *So Betty Botter bought a bit of better butter.*

According to researchers at MIT, the most difficult tongue twister is "pad kid poured curd pulled cod."[10] I actually find that one quite easy – maybe it's an accent thing. The toughest tongue twister according to the *Guinness Book of World Records* is more challenging: "The sixth sick sheik's sixth sheep's sick."[11]

If you can spin out a few fancy tongue twisters,

you'll find your presentations and speeches will roll off the tongue!

3. Do a daily voice warm-up

Make speaking with clarity a habit, not an occasional effort. Bring your articulation into unconscious competence by warming up every single day, regardless of whether you're public speaking or not. The shower is a great place to habit stack this one, as the steam helps open the vocal channel.

Here's an easy five-step warm-up you can use, including exercises we've covered so far:

1. **Angry Librarian:** breathe low and deep into the tummy and exhale on the sound "sh!" for as long as you can.
2. **Bumble-Bee Breathing:** exhale on a "hummm." Can you feel the vibrations in your heart space?
3. **Braying Horse:** vibrate your lips like "brrr." Can you change the pitch as you do this?
4. **Surprised Donkey:** say *"ee-aw-ah"* while stretching the lips and jaw as wide as you can.
5. **Tongue Twisters:** Whip out your favourite tongue twister, Shakespearean monologue, or

line from the presentation you have that day.

Important public service announcement: Speaking with clarity does not mean. Enunciating. Every. Single. Word.

If you sound out every word, you'll come across as stilted and robotic. A natural speech rhythm brings out the words that matter, and the rest are just connectors. There are stars of the show and the supporting cast. For example, in the above line: *stars, show, supporting* and *cast* need to be emphasised, but *there, are, of, the, and* can almost be skipped over.

And now for the answer you've all been waiting for … Well maybe not, but I do get asked this question a lot: **How do I stop saying "um" and "ah"?**

Let me preface this by saying I am not the "um" and "ah" police. Fluency with a few fillers is much better than sounding mechanical with no fillers. The goal is to speak with filler-free fluency.

What's your filler of choice?
Um, ah, sort of, like, you know, actually, literally, obviously? Let me know on socials using #fillerofchoice.

Why do you use fillers?
There are three main reasons:
1. **Lack of preparation,** so you're caught off guard.
2. **An inner voice is distracting you,** so you're not focused on what you're saying.
3. **You're afraid to pause,** so instead of taking a breath, you fill the silence with a filler.

In all three scenarios, it's like you have a lotto ball barrel of thoughts above your head, and the balls either get stuck on the way out, or hurtle out like a rogue tennis ball machine. Try this simple yet powerful technique:

The Ball-Drop Voice-Follow
Rather than those lotto balls flying out of your mouth uncontrollably or getting jammed, breathe and pause and wait for them to gather in the rail as a train of thought *before* you speak. Balls drop first; voice follows second. This helps you slow down, gather your words, and share them with confidence as a complete thought.

In other words, have a filter and use it.

**Above all, remember to relax.
Tension is the enemy
of fluent speech.**

The more pressure you put on yourself to be 'polished', the more blocks you'll place in the way. Besides, polished and perfect may not have the effect you want.

In one of my early webinars, I was taking students through the Rag Doll exercise, which is brilliant for posture and alignment. If you practise yoga, you'll be all over this. It's where you hang your head between your legs in a forward fold and then slowly rebuild your spine …

"Vertebrae bry bertebrae. Sorry, I mean verterbrae bry brerter –" *Dammit!*

For the life of me, I could not get the words out – *vertebrae by vertebrae*. In that moment, I thought my business was done for. *A speaking coach who can't even speak properly?*

Then much to my surprise, someone unmuted on the call and said, "Oh my gosh, Sally, you're live?"

I was baffled. "Yes, I'm here, hello."

"You always speak so perfectly I thought you must have prerecorded it! Good to know you're a real person who makes mistakes!"

That webinar was a big 'aha' moment.

> **People don't want flawless;**
> **they want realness.**

So please, do your speech exercises and elevate your articulation, but embark on this clarity quest with playfulness, not perfection. At best you'll wow your audience with impeccable enunciation, and at worst you come away with a champagne and a brilliant anecdote *wink*.

YOUR CLARITY AFFIRMATION
"I speak with clarity and ease."

"People don't want flawless,
they want realness."

SALLY PROSSER

"A speaker who does not strike oil in ten minutes should stop boring."

LOUIS NIZER

CHAPTER 12
E = EXPRESSION

Ding. New Instagram DM.

> *This might sound strange, but I think you and your partner are in today's Hobart Mercury.*

As a former journalist, I'm no stranger to headlines, but this message from an Insta-acquaintance takes the birthday suit cake.

I rang Patrick immediately.

"Get online and look for the *Hobart Mercury*." I was quite firm.

"Oh. My. God."

There we were – one arm around each other's waist and the other scooping the air making a big U shape. We formed the U in *Mercury* on the front page.

And did I mention we were butt naked?

No claim to shame. This was our claim to fame.

Each June, people get nude and brave the waters of Sandy Bay in Hobart at sunrise to mark the winter solstice. In 2023, it was a clear, chilly morning. Red swim caps, white towels, and the air thick with anticipation.

Then came the drums. *Boom. Boom-Boom.*

Get ready to strip and dip. *Boom. Boom-Boom.*

Up went the bright red flares, and the starting horn blared across the beach. We're off! The playful shrieks of 2,000 naked people scrambling into the water filled the dawn.

I was transported back to my surf life saving days and hit the lead – in what was *not* a race. After the snowy mountains expedition, this was a summer swim for me. My form was great; my smile was big, and I even high-fived the lifeguard straddling his board at the turn-around point. He wasn't getting paid enough for that job – or getting paid too much – it's all a matter of perspective on my perky pair of floaties.

By the time we made it back to the beach, most people had stripped, dipped and dashed. After warming our bits by the fire drums with the faithful few remaining, we wanted to record the wild moment. A spirited woman grabbed my iPhone, and Patrick and I headed for the shallows to be artistically silhouetted by the rising sun.

"Great shot!" she said, handing back the phone.

She wasn't alone in thinking this. Little did we know, a photographer from the state's premier newspaper also papped our peaches. When the marketing gurus suggested getting exposure for my business, I doubt *this* was what they had in mind.

So, we did what anyone would do in our situation. Ordered the image, blew it up, printed it, framed it and stuck it in the entrance way of our apartment.

Look, it's not the *first* thing you see when you walk in … If you're Brisbane-based and want an in-person private session, you'll get to see it.

That front-page moment isn't just a crazy story I hope gave you a chuckle. It was about full-bodied, unbridled self-expression. And that's exactly what your voice needs to do: strip back hesitation, dive in and own the moment.

If I had any remnants of fearing the judgement of others, I shed them with my little white towel on that sand and gave it the proverbial middle finger with a front-page mooning.

Just to be clear: **you don't need to get your gear off to show us your voiceprint.**

But that feeling of freedom and fun with a splash of wild woman or man is exactly the expressive sensation you want to feel when sharing your voice. Bare it all! Imagine Madonna in your ears – "Express yourself!"

> **It's the perfect anthem for the final element of the V.O.I.C.E Formula, E for EXPRESSION.**

Expression is the last piece of the Style Voiceprint puzzle – and for good reason. If you've followed everything up to this point, your voice will already be brimming with natural expression. When your voice clicks into alignment with the meaning of what you're saying – your audience becomes immersed in your message. They hang on every word.

> *Manner* **needs to match** *matter*;
> **the** *how* **needs to match the** *what.*

The Three Ps of Expression are pitch, pace and power.
- **Pitch** – High to low. The note of your voice.
- **Pace** – Fast to slow. The rate of your speech.
- **Power** – Loud to soft. The volume of your sound.

PITCH

Cue the yawn and let's take a painful trip to Monotone Town. Where everyone speaks on the same note. No matter what they say. And your challenge is to stay awake; otherwise you'll get stranded in that boring borough where expression goes to die. Monotone Town sounds like a pretty dismal destination. You don't want to be posted there permanently!

If you speak on a single note, it's like pounding the same xylophone bar over and over and over – it does your head in! But when you explore your full vocal range, you create an engaging, dynamic, and captivating performance – and you'd definitely get kicked off the Monotone Town payroll!

How do you vary your pitch?

The good news is you don't need to be able to sing

'Do-Re-Mi' like Julie Andrews in *The Sound of Music;* you just need to be able to go *up* and *down*. Say this out loud with me: I can speak *high*! I can speak lowww. Feel the difference? That's your pitch range in action.

We touched on this in the Vibrations chapter. Your pitch is higher when the vibrations are positioned in the head, lower in the heart space and lower again in the solar plexus. Remember, head for *think*, heart for *feel* and solar plexus for *do*.

You can also **let the words be your guide.**

What words and phrases lend themselves to a higher pitch? I'm thinking:

- Big picture
- Wonder/Ponder
- Vision/Planning
- Creative/Out-of-the-box
- Brainstorm/Ideas
- High/Tall/Increase
- Sun/Sky/Clouds

What words lend themselves to a lower pitch? I've landed on:

- Dragging your feet/rock bottom
- Mother Earth/grounded

- Low/decrease
- Debrief
- Deep in my bones
- Foundations/floor
- Let's dive into the details

It's so simple when you let the words be your guide – they tell you what pitch to use! And when in doubt, start low so you have somewhere to go.

PACE

One of the biggest speaking myths is that slow speech is good speech. You know the voice I'm talking about. Think school assembly or awards night. Where everything. Is nice. And clear. But it sounds. Like a metronome. Lulling you into a trance of boredom. Very different to the Lulling Effect we covered in the Intonation chapter!

How to keep pace?

There are three ways you can change the pace of your voice:

1. Elongate or truncate the vowel sounds in the words. Think of making the words big and fat or short and sharp.

2. Take more frequent pauses.
3. Take longer pauses.

Is it better to speak fast or slow?

Some studies show faster talkers are perceived as more persuasive and competent.[12] At the same time, speaking too fast can make you sound nervous, like you're chasing your words.

There are also studies that show people who pause before answering questions are more charismatic, because it shows thoughtfulness.[13] Taking big pauses also creates suspense — that's why the Tease and Land intonation pattern works so brilliantly.

The verdict? Fast talkers come across as energetic and confident — until they outrun their point. If you never slow down, you risk overwhelming your audience. Slow talkers come across as thoughtful and poised — until they grind to a halt. If you never speed up, you risk putting your audience to sleep.

The secret? Vary your speed. It's not about speaking fast *or* slow; it's about being able to speak fast *and* slow. Again, look to the meaning and intention of the words to be your guide. If you were telling a story about racing to catch the bus, you wouldn't deliver it slowly.

Likewise, a story about a sloth moving 3 metres a day would sound weird if spoken quickly.

Also, slow down when sharing concepts that are new to the audience. When I was a TV news reporter, I covered an incredible story about the world's first mini kidney grown in a lab. This extraordinary discovery paves the way for one day growing a full-sized kidney, ending the agonising wait for a transplant. When the researcher was telling us about this in the interview, he spoke so quickly and non-expressively you'd think he was telling us where to find a car park!

On the other hand, some motivational speakers say the most overdone, banal one-liners, but they deliver their message so well people are crying in their seats and shouting from the stands! *Turn your mess into your message! The power is within* you!

POWER

"Can you hear me up the back?"

Most speaking coaches will tell you this is a terrible way to start a speech. And sure, it's not the most riveting opening, but here's the thing: the most riveting opening won't have any impact if people can't hear you.

That's why I always suggest using a microphone if one is available. Resisting a microphone isn't about toughness or your comfort – it's about prioritising your audience. Take the focus off you and your self-diagnosed loud voice and think of audience members who might be hard of hearing. In my experience, speakers grossly overestimate their audibility, especially in rooms with poor acoustics. Even trained actors can't compete with bad acoustics. Plus, using a microphone allows you to employ the underrated technique of decreasing your volume.

How do you crank up the volume?
The volume of your voice is controlled by the intensity of airflow, which increases the intensity of vibrations.

I have vivid memories from primary school of being screamed at by a young teacher because we weren't lining up after the recess break. I was a star student who really liked this teacher, so I was quiet and in line, but none of the other kids seemed to pay any attention. Her face was getting redder; her temper was getting shorter, and her voice was getting hoarser.

"*Year two*, QUIET! Get in line and listen to your teacher!"

The voice carried from the neighbouring classroom like a sound from another realm. The kids stopped talking and got immediately in line.

The difference? Teacher One was forcing. She was screeching. All the energy was coming from her throat and head. Her voice was miles away from her diaphragm and completely lacked carrying power. Teacher Two commanded from the solar plexus; her voice carried, and the message was heard.

So, if you want to increase volume, don't increase force, increase airflow. Take in a deeper lower breath and let your words ride out on a wave of supported air.

As with pitch and pace, words can guide the way you use volume. A 'huge bang' would be loud, while a secret would be soft. You might be getting flashbacks to high school English lessons here with the way we're using onomatopoeia – making something sound like what it is. For example: bang, splash, creak.

Take this a step further and use the Three Ps of pitch, pace and power to set or shift the temperature of a room. Negotiations getting heated? No worries, cool it down with a lower pitch, slower pace, softer volume and stay still with your body. Walked into an icy room of disengaged eyes? Warm it up with a higher pitch, faster pace, louder volume and move around the room using gestures.

> ## EXERCISE
> ### Gibberish
>
> - Let's get weird. Pick a random emotion, for example, excited, annoyed, mysterious.
> - Now talk in gibberish like you really mean it. Go 'nude swim' big! Play with pitch, pace and power.
> - If you're not laughing, you're not trying hard enough!
>
> If you have the audiobook, you'll hear my particular flavour of gibberish.

Letting go of structured language and focusing purely on *how* you talk rather than *what* you say is an incredible way to embody emotion without hiding behind words. Because the more your voice flows and the more fun you're having, the more expressive you'll sound.

Imbue your words with aligned vibrations, openness, intonation, clarity and expression, and your stylish voiceprint will make front page news.

> **YOUR EXPRESSION AFFIRMATION**
> "My voice expresses the meaning of my message."

PART TWO

YOUR V.O.I.C.E AFFIRMATIONS

I have the power to
bring the good vibes.

I am open and
ready to receive.

I trust in the musical
flow of my voice.

I speak with clarity
and ease.

My voice expresses
the meaning of
my message.

Quick check-in: How are you feeling?

Did the V.O.I.C.E Formula send you into a spin – arms and legs flailing in random directions? It's a lot to take in, and as I mentioned earlier, you're not meant to master it all at once. The best speakers had to start somewhere.

Have fun experimenting with the exercises and techniques – and watch what happens. Watch people pay attention when you speak, hear the resonant power in your voice and feel confidence like you've never experienced before.

> **Words on a page can guide you, but voice-to-voice is where real transformation happens.**

If you're ready to take the next step, I'd love to welcome you to *Soul Speakers* – my online community where we go deeper into what it truly takes to become a confident, compelling speaker. It's a safe, supportive space to learn, practise and receive real-time feedback from me – all while leading from your heart and soul!

Your voice is a valuable asset, and now it's time to *invest* in it.

PART THREE

INVEST IN YOUR VOICEPRINT

"Craft your life blueprint with your voiceprint."

SALLY PROSSER

CHAPTER 13
SPEAK YOUR BLUEPRINT

"Thank you, God," I whispered to the sky.

Then I reeled in my fishing line, placed the rod in its holder and lay on the esky in the middle of the boat to read my *Baby-Sitters Club* book.

"What are you doing, Sal? The fish are biting!" My dad was confused.

Resting the book on my chest, I turned to Dad with calm conviction. "I prayed for five carp on this trip – and I got my five."

I was a pious little 9-year-old.

Dad chuckled, shrugged his shoulders and dined out on that anecdote for years.

I was a manifesting baddie long before I knew the

M word. Actually, we're all manifesters – some of us are just *conscious* of it.

Ready to call in what you want?
Start by calling it out with your voice! You can't attract what you won't articulate.

> Gandhi said it best:
> *Carefully watch your thoughts, for*
> *they become your words.*
> **Manage and watch your words,**
> **for they will become your actions.**
> *Consider and judge your actions, for*
> *they become your habits.*
> *Acknowledge and watch your habits, for*
> *they shall become your values.*
> *Understand and embrace your values,*
> *for they become your destiny.*

The way you speak, to yourself and others, has a direct impact on your experience of reality. The words we speak cast spells into the world. In fact, the word *abracadabra* comes from the Aramaic or Hebrew phrase meaning, "I create as I speak."

You can craft your life blueprint with your voiceprint – or at least ensure you're on the best timeline for your soul's journey.

This lesson dawned on me after the fake doctor saga and a slew of subsequent men who weren't right for me. So, I decided to write down everything I wanted in a relationship – in detail – and voicerecorded it with expression.

Please note, this was after I cried, complained, and drank my body weight in wine for many months straight. Circa 2016, I would find myself washing my hair in the shower, and out of my mouth the words involuntarily tumbled, "Fuck, I hate men. Men are the worst." Before I knew better, my friends and I would enjoy what we called a *prosecco haze* (many hours and many bottles) and mutter, "Maaate men! All psychopaths, narcissists, misogynists." It was a man-hating tipsy tongue twister.

Yet, I *really* wanted to meet my person. How on Earth was I *not* finding a loving, non-narcissistic, non-psychopathic man amid all this?! Riddle me that.

It all came to a head when a new squeeze invited me on a romantic weekend away. My imagination ran wild with silly fantasies of forever, and my bag was packed a day early. The night before we were supposed to leave, he rang me: "Yeah, Sal, I realised I don't really like you, so we're not going anymore."

Ouch. Rejection. I sobbed over the lonely bag at the end of my bed and felt Taylor Swift's lyrics viscerally: "Casually cruel in the name of being honest."

But if I was truly being honest with myself, I was cut-up about a guy *I* didn't even really like – he had too much ego and far too many little kids. He wasn't at all what I was looking for. And it became abundantly clear that I had nothing clear.

In defence of all the men who dumped me, I was a steaming hot mess with far too much crazy on the hot-to-crazy ratio. If I wanted to date a man with his shit together, I had to get mine sorted. And the degrees, the job, the property and the Pilates-body didn't count. I had to go deeper into who I was.

So that's when I sat at my kitchen table, broke out a new journal and fancy pens, and laid it bare on the page: *Title: My ideal relationship.* Not as a list, as a story in the present tense. *I am so happy and grateful to be in a relationship with a person who is …* It included facts and *feelings*. For example, instead of *he prioritises me,* I wrote

I feel so safe around him because I know he puts me first.

After I was happy with the two-and-a-half-page script, it needed to be signed, sealed and delivered with my voiceprint. A contract vibrating with the emotion of my future self. As if that man on paper was in the reality of right now.

I recorded it on my phone, and it became my new audio-obsession. I played it around the clock – with morning make-up, afternoon jigsaw puzzling and night skincare routines.

For a while I was feeling really great. My business was gathering early momentum at the time, so stepping into my coaching queendom helped me stay more positive about dating. I was no longer convulsively cursing men in the shower. My future-self story seeped into my prosecco-soaked pores, and I would even dramatically perform it aloud on occasion, like I was back auditioning for a Shakespearean play.

I lived alone; I could do this weird stuff.

And this is how you can do it too.

PART THREE

EXERCISE
How to Manifest with Your Voice

1. Write a *story*, not a list

- **Use *present* tense** – I *am* rather than I *want*. Saying *want* will keep you in the energy of wanting, not having.
- **Use *positive* language** – the unconscious mind doesn't process negatives, so write what you *do* want, not what you *don't*.
- **Include facts and *feelings*** – how do you *feel* having these things in your life?
- **Use *your* language** – words and phrases you ordinarily use.
- **Call in your *future self*** – imagine the future version of yourself describing your life to you.

2. *Record* it with vocal *expression*

- Voicerecord or videorecord the story to your phone.
- Immerse yourself in the feelings of the story physically, emotionally and vocally.
- Use variation in pitch, pace, volume, inflection, pausing, facial expression and gesture.

> **3. *Play* it back often**
> - Embed this audio into your subconscious by playing it last thing at night and first thing in the morning. Play it while you're getting ready, cooking, doing housework, and so on until it nestles like a song you can't get out of your head.
>
> **4. *Perform* it like you mean it**
> - Memorise the story.
> - Perform it around the house with the same vigour with which you recorded it. Better yet, increase the vigour.
> - Always ensure that story is top of mind for you.

The way you deliver your manifestation matters.

It's well understood that the way you feel impacts the way you speak. You can tell if a friend is down just by the way they answer the phone. It also works the other way around – the way you *speak* affects the way you *feel*. If you express yourself in a joyful way, you will feel more joy.[1]

PART THREE

With all this wisdom, I wish I could tell you I was a perfect little manifesting baddie. Turns out, I'm human. Some days, the pull to drink a buttery chardonnay in the bath while cranking sad country ballads violently took over.

One post-pity party bath, the universe sent me a podcast from Kathrin Zenkina – who's better known as Manifestation Babe. It was the first time I'd listened to any of her content. Kathrin shared the quite incredible story of how she met her now husband on Tinder.

Her words pinged like a red flame notification in my head.

I was a dating app early adopter. I had them all back in the day when Tinder was purely a hook-up app and even Blendr existed. At the time I heard the podcast, I was only on Bumble and Hinge. The Manifestation Babe inspired me to re-download Tinder. What the hell, I was overdue a bit of action, and hey, you never know ...

Almost immediately, I matched with Patrick.

It wasn't love at first swipe. But he looked like he knew what he was doing, and I hadn't seen him on any other app, which said a lot – the Brisbane pool was small. I later found out he'd only downloaded Tinder

2 weeks prior and didn't even know any other dating apps existed.

Then I did something very out of character. I went for a morning coffee date. My usual pattern was a game of 'how many wines do I need to make this evening mildly interesting?' But I'd spoken at a university breakfast function so was up early and had a reason to blow-dry my hair. It was one of my first gigs. I got excellent feedback and $900, so my confidence was through the roof.

I waited patiently by a public bike rack in nude stilettos, navy capris, a white peplum top and gold-rimmed aviator sunglasses.

"Did you ride here?" It was a cute opening line.

I just glared. It was too early to tell if he had a sense of humour or was an idiot.

Then, according to Patrick, I didn't walk, I floated alongside him to the cafe.

A few more coffees, multiple sleepovers and an overseas trip together took us to the 4-month milestone. That's when I stumbled across that old document, my Man Manifesto, and I'm not joking – every single thing I wrote in that two-and-a-half pages of specifics was true.

PART THREE

I have no doubt the activity of writing it, voicing it, recording it, listening to it and even performing it – submitted the order to the universe. And gosh did She deliver. There is no way a stable man like Patrick, who is crystal clear on what he wants, would have come into my world if I was the woman saying "I hate men" every day.

So, you might be thinking: *Sweet story. Sounds like a far-fetched coincidence.*

That would've been my dad. If he knew I was writing a chapter about manifesting with your voice, he'd roll his eyes. He was a very facts-and-data kinda guy, none of this wishy-washy touchy-feely palava.

"But Dad!" I'd say, "there *are* facts and data behind this."

There's a wealth of research across psychology, neuroscience, linguistics, and even quantum physics that supports the idea that the words we speak and how we speak them influence our reality.

The theory of Hebbian learning (Hebb's rule) states "neurons that fire together, wire together." Repeated speech patterns reinforce neural pathways in the brain, shaping thoughts, behaviours, and perceptions of reality.

When Dad wasn't telling the story of the five carp I prayed for, he'd boast about the fishing trip that same year where I caught an Australian record yellowbelly while trolling the wall of Glenbawn Dam in Northern New South Wales.

It was 7.7 kilograms and fed my family of six for weeks. The scientific name for a yellowbelly fish species is *Macquaria ambigua* – and that took no research! Growing up, Dad made us recite the scientific name of any fish before we ate it – those neural pathways are wired together with zip ties. Along with every word to the bridge in Savage Garden's song 'I Want You', which I belted in my car on repeat. *Sweet like a chic-a-cherry cola.* Both pieces of information are exceptionally useful in my everyday life, as you can imagine!

The reticular activating system (RAS) in the brain filters information and prioritises what aligns with our spoken thoughts and beliefs. If we repeatedly say, "I'm terrible at public speaking" or, "I hate all men," the RAS will highlight experiences reinforcing that belief.

Words wield power.

You've probably heard of the placebo effect, but what about its evil brother the **'nocebo effect'?**[2] If a doctor says, "You have six months to live," the body often aligns with that belief. Speaking your blueprint can be a matter of life or death.

The vibrations of our voice affect the vibrations of everything around us.

Dr Masaru Emoto's water crystal experiments are fascinating. He found that words and intentions change the molecular structure of water. Water exposed to positive words and intentions formed beautiful, symmetrical crystalline structures when frozen, while water exposed to negative words and intentions formed chaotic, asymmetrical patterns.[3] Given humans are at *least* 60 percent water, it makes sense that spoken words affect us on a cellular level.

It's the **universal law of resonance:** the rate of vibration projected will harmonise with and attract back energies with the same resonance. We get what we give! Have you heard yourself say these phrases?

- "I've always been a bad public speaker, and it never gets easier."

- "I hate that I have to show up on social media for my business."
- "I should get some help with my speech, but expensive coaching isn't for me."

If you say so.

Remember Gandhi – *Manage and watch your words, for they will become your actions.*

Seven language shifts to speak a better future

1. Avoid *always* and *never*, unless it's something you always or never want to do.

2. Replace I "have to" with I "get to."

3. Accept compliments graciously.

4. Replace I "should" with I "choose to."

5. Say "I'm learning" instead of "I'm bad at this."

6. Replace "I'm busy" with "I'm prioritising."

7. Say "how can I?" instead of "I can't."

PART THREE

And don't be all talk and no action!

"Sal, you're so lucky! *How* did you get that?!"

An acquaintance from university was surprised to hear me reading the news on the local radio station and approached me one day after class. She assumed I knew someone or my parents knew someone or I just got a phone call out of the blue.

"I rang the radio station."

She looked baffled. "How did you get the number?"

"I looked it up in the phone book." This was before the days of Google.

"And how did you know what to say?" No wonder she was studying journalism – all the questions!

The truth is I was extremely nervous and didn't know what to say, but I winged it and asked the receptionist if I could speak to the newsroom. Next thing, I was invited in to meet the news director, which led to work experience, which led to a job.

There are two types of people.

Type one: those who make up stories about why other people succeed – and excuses for why they can't.

Type two: those who get out there and make it

happen. They work with what they've got. They ask, and they act.

Type one waits for the fish to bite, and type two manifests the fish they catch.

Out on that boat as a kid, I had no idea what 'manifestation' was. But I knew how to say my prayers out loud and trusted they'd be answered. Turns out, I had it pretty sorted. Manifestation is intention plus action. So, make sure you take action to match your voice – and don't underestimate the power of just *asking*.

Ready to speak your dream life into existence?

If you say so.

"What you do today impacts your sound tomorrow."

SALLY PROSSER

CHAPTER 14
PROLONG YOUR PRINT

Every now and then, I get a client like Mary.

Most of my clients reach out to prepare for a speech, grow their business or clear a throat chakra blockage. But Mary wasn't most clients. Mary was in her 70s – a doting grandmother, a proud parishioner and physically losing her voice. She loved doing Bible readings at church but was getting replaced on the roster because her voice was giving way mid Prayers of the Faithful. She loved connecting with her grandkids but couldn't hold their attention on the phone because they couldn't *hear* her. Mary's voiceprint was fading – and with it her confidence and human connections. If you got a pang of voice-gratitude reading this. Bottle that feeling.

PART THREE

Your voice is like any part of the physical body – if you want it to stay functional, you need to take care of it.

Five ways time takes its toll on your voiceprint

1. **Your voice weakens.** Loss of vocal cord muscle (atrophy) makes it harder to project.

2. **Your pitch control fades.** Because your vocal cords become less flexible.

3. **Your voice sounds hoarse.** Poor mucus production means the vocal cords are less lubricated, leading to a rough, raspy voice.

4. **You become harder to hear.** Declining lung capacity and diaphragm strength mean you lose breath support for speaking.

5. **You struggle to articulate.** Tongue and lip muscles lose precision.

The good news is you can prevent this happening with quality coaching and proper care. We know doing consistent exercise pays dividends in the health of your future body. Are you looking after your future voice?

> **Five ways to keep your voice strong**
>
> 1. **Do daily voice warm-ups**
>   Not warming up your voice before speaking is like breaking into a sprint without stretching, or grabbing the heaviest weight as soon as you walk in the gym.
>
>   Just like those examples, if you don't warm up, you're going to do yourself an injury – likely one that compounds over time. There are some great exercises in the Clarity chapter.
>
> 2. **Use the right breathing technique**
>   Hold your hand in front of your lips and talk. Feel that warm airflow? This is what we want. If the air is not flowing freely, chances are you're forcing it, and this is going to inflame your vocal cords.
>
>   Revisit the Ground and Breathe chapter.
>
> 3. **Drink enough water**
>   Your body needs to be hydrated for your

vocal cords to function properly. Warm water or herbal tea is best. Remember, caffeine and alcohol dehydrate.

4. Take enough rest

Even the world's fittest people can't exercise nonstop. Athletes are often hardcore resting when they're not hardcore training.

When I'm scheduling my speaking, workshops and live coaching, I always intentionally plan for rest. For example, if I've been running a full-day workshop, I won't book clients that evening.

5. Express your emotions

Recurring voice issues are a sign your throat chakra is blocked. A key to clearing the blockage and getting this energetic centre healthy is to verbalise things you've unconsciously stuffed down. It's like clearing the energetic pipes – moving the e-motions, that energy in motion.

I helped Mary with all these techniques, especially the warm-up exercises to strengthen her vocal cords. It definitely made a difference, and her vocal endurance improved. Unfortunately, by the time the voice is waning, it's very challenging to bring it back – even with specialised medical intervention.

**Don't wait for the inkpad to run dry
before you start conserving it.**

If you want your voice to stand the test of time, you need to invest in it. Otherwise, like an abandoned grand piano gathering dust, your voiceprint will fade into non-existence – and you'll be coughing up regret from neglect.

**What you do today impacts
your sound tomorrow.**

A secret hope of mine, is that #prolongtheprint will start trending. Wouldn't it be fabulous to see people loudly and proudly caring for their voice?!

If I'm yet to inspire you to take charge of your voice for *yourself*, please do it for the sake of others. What would you give to hear the voice of someone you loved and lost? Maybe you're lucky enough to have that recording. Leave that audio gift on Earth.

Prolonging your voiceprint isn't just about *your* lifetime.
Your voice is loaded and coded with intergenerational messaging. Your voice holds the song of your grandmother, the pain of your father, and the cry of your children. It holds codes AI can never replicate – because your voice is uniquely human.

Your voice is auditory DNA.
When we speak, we carry the vocal torch of those before us and hand it on to those after us. Remember, that could be the unwanted baton of trauma. Losing your voice isn't always about aging. Sometimes we inherit silence – sewn into us before we can even speak.

- *Don't speak unless spoken to.*
- *Keep your emotions in check.*
- *Don't draw attention to yourself.*

These mantras echo through generations. People

raised in environments where emotions weren't freely expressed may inherit a flat, constrained or overly cautious way of speaking. When past generations have been punished for speaking up, their descendants often carry an unconscious anxiety around being heard. This isn't just emotional; it's embodied. Trauma lives in the breath, the diaphragm, the throat. It constricts vocal freedom, tightens tone and limits projection.[4] I can hear it.

A cycle of secrets, shame and unspoken truths settles like sediment in your voiceprint. You may not even realise you're carrying the weight of someone else's silence, because it sounds like:

- *Keep the peace.*
- *Don't dredge up the past.*
- *What happens in this house stays in this house.*
- *Don't bring shame on the family.*
- *Don't air our dirty laundry.*
- *Why can't you just move on?*

These phrases masquerade as love or loyalty, but they muffle truth, perpetuate harm and create the kind of vocal tension I help people unwind.

PART THREE

One of my clients, Shae, described it as suffocating in a prison built from her own silence. Shae was born in Korea and adopted by an Australian family with a culture of secrecy. This not only meant Shae felt disconnected from her identity, but speaking up felt like betrayal.

When we began working together, she wouldn't post any face-to-camera content. By the time we finished, she was publicly sharing her adoption story with courage and clarity. Shae shattered the silence, broke the family pattern and became a catalyst for meaningful change. Now, she's being invited on podcasts, and fellow adult adoptees message her with gratitude. And her boys are watching. Shae has healed forward and backward through her lineage.

Shae said in one of our many voice notes: "Sometimes there are still shadows inside me that are like, *'Oh Shae, you don't want to expose all your private information to people,'* and then I remember what you said – **'It's not a violation of privacy, it's a reclamation of power.'** That has really stuck with me."

Another incredible truth-teller Katie Delimon is lighting the way by speaking up and healing generational pain. She's shared publicly about discovering that her brother was adopted, her aunt was murdered, and her biological father wasn't the man who raised her. Katie says, "You're not damaging the family by speaking up, you're acknowledging the damage that's *already* been done and offering a chance to heal."[5]

> **Speaking your truth doesn't
> break the family.
> It breaks the silence that's
> been breaking you.**

Psychiatrist Dr Dan Siegel reminds us, "Name it to tame it." And Brené Brown, in one of my favourite quotes of all time, says: "Shame cannot survive being spoken. It cannot tolerate having words wrapped around it."

What are your family voice blocks? How can you shift the sound of future generations?

Because when you pioneer the change by speaking – you don't just free your own voice; you redefine the family voiceprint.

PART THREE

Break the bad, prolong the positive.
Remember, every dark attribute has a light side. It can be easy to get snagged on all the trauma and forget to celebrate generational gifts.

> **Take time to recognise the parts of your family voiceprint you want to amplify as your legacy.**

My dad was at times abrasive when making his opinions heard, but thanks to that, I've never had an issue speaking up for myself. He gave great speeches at our family birthdays and weddings, so picking up a microphone felt as natural as picking up a glass of water for me from a young age.

Mum can talk to anyone and makes friends quickly. I remember being in a department store as a kid trying on clothes in the fitting room. When I came out, she was having a deep conversation with a sales assistant.

"Do you know each other?" I asked.

"Oh, this is Kate. We just met while you were putting the dress on." For Mum, this was a normal occurrence.

I'm proud to continue the legacy of strong communicators, and just by being who I am and running the business I do, I'm showing my nieces and nephews how to use their voice.

What family voiceprint do you vow to carry on?
Your voice lights the vocal confidence and courage of your whole lineage. You're not just speaking for yourself – you're speaking for your ancestors, your descendants and everyone in between.

Prolong your voiceprint for you.

Prolong your voiceprint for them.

"Your voice is your access-all-areas pass."

SALLY PROSSER

CHAPTER 15
ACCESS ALL AREAS

"Good morning. Thanks for coming."

I looked out to a sea of faces. None looked happy. Every seat was taken, and people were standing crammed against the back wall. My heart was pounding through my mouth. I couldn't breathe. Feeling my sister's shoulder pressed against mine, I somehow found air.

"A place ..." My voice cracked. I locked eyes with Mum. *What was the point of all those bloody speech and drama lessons if I can't keep it together in a moment like this?!*

I closed my eyes and heard Dad's voice. *Come on, Sal.* Flashbacks of us in his fishing boat laughing over baked bean jaffles and corn kernel burley drifted into focus.

I took another breath, tasting the salty sea air.

Then I opened my eyes with a gentle nudge from my sister, and spoke.

PART THREE

"'A place for everything and everything in its place.' This was Dad's favourite saying. And as I look out on all of you, I can see he found a place in so many lives."

My dad, John Charles Prosser, died on 23 January 2014. His eulogy stands as the hardest speaking gig I've ever had to do. It also stands as the most meaningful.

> **Why bother with all this voiceprint stuff if you can't use it in life's moments that really matter? If you can't speak for the people you love and the causes you care about?**

Because *this* is what your voice is for.

Speaking is a verb, not a noun. Sorry (not sorry) to hit you with a high school English stick. Speaking isn't just a *thing* you do; it's an *action* you take. You're transporting a message and *choosing* your voice as the vehicle to deliver it – and why wouldn't you?

Your voice is wired with connection codes that no email, no slide deck, no printed agenda can replicate. You *feel* the eulogy more than the booklet. You *remember* the apology, the pitch, the toast for *how* it was said. And sure, I get it – some meetings should have been an email. But the ones that matter? The ones that change minds, move hearts or mark a moment? They need a voice. A voice fit for the job.

This is the real power of a strong, versatile voiceprint. Just like a fingerprint scanner unlocks doors, your voiceprint opens up access to people, places and possibilities. The more you invest in your voice – the higher security clearance you'll have, and the more adaptable you'll become.

Tragically, 10 years after Dad died, my mum lost her second husband, Gaz, in a horrific light plane crash. I was given the task of hosting his celebration of life service. It was a tumultuous, emotionally intense time. The calendar meant that the night before the memorial, I gave a lighthearted keynote to 200 teenagers at a university. I have no doubt the reason I was able to switch gears so dramatically is thanks to my voice and communication training.

Can you switch communication gears? Or are you stuck on the default setting?

In NLP (neurolinguistic programming), there's a presupposition that "the person with the greatest flexibility of behaviour rules the system." It essentially means the individual who's most adaptable will have

PART THREE

the most control over the outcome or dynamics in any given situation. This is particularly true when it comes to the way you speak.

I once had someone say to me: "This is how I fuckin' speak. You can like it or lump it." Look, I'm all for confidence and security in who you are – absolutely! But declaring your voice only strikes one note is small-minded and stunts your influence.

"I'll tell you what your strength is: you can talk to the CEO as effectively as you talk to the front line." This peer feedback was given to my client who's a general manager at a large company. Her job can involve hosting the prime minister on the same day as speaking to the media, running a leadership meeting, connecting with entry-level workers and negotiating with her kids. When I asked her what she made of the feedback, she said, "Well it's about trust, isn't it? You need to be able to communicate to a broad range of people if you want them to trust you. And if they don't trust you, how the hell are you supposed to get anything done or changed?!"

That's voiceprint intelligence – the ability to shift your delivery on purpose.

People feel like you *get* them because you're attuned to where you are and who you're speaking to. It's about reading the room and rising to meet it. It's about having the access-all-areas pass on your voiceprint and choosing what the moment calls for.

Think of it like your wardrobe. If you're always using your default voice, it's like wearing the same outfit every day. Let's say it's a cute activewear set – perfect for the gym, a walk, or even a work-from-home day at a pinch. Now picture rocking up to a business meeting or a black-tie ball in the same thing. Sure, you're comfy, but unless you're spruiking something sporty, you're not exactly dressed to impress.

> **Expand and curate your voice wardrobe so you have range to choose from – and you serve your vocal realness every single time.**

It means you can take your voice from the stage to the social media scroll, from the bowling club to the boardroom, from the podcast to the pub, from the workshop to the wedding speech.

My speaking skills have taken me from eisteddfod

stages as a teenager to entertainment centre stages as an adult. From spruiking $20 cardigans in a mall to recording voiceovers for hair salon ads across the state. From radio news bulletins in regional Australia to live crosses for national TV news broadcasters.

Gosh, I remember in the 2013 Rockhampton floods, dragging heavy sandbags against the house while my friend, with his rifle, guarded me from brown snakes seeking higher ground. One hour later, I was in the newsroom with thongs down below and business attire up top live-crossing to Brisbane about a dangerous floodwater helicopter rescue. This doesn't compare to the vocal ninja work I did a few years later.

It all started at the Battle of Brisbane – a professional boxing match between Manny Pacquiao and Jeff Horn – held at a major stadium. From the moment my friend and I took our seats, the heckling began from the guy behind us. Drunk and disruptive became offensive and then downright abusive. My editor said I couldn't put it in the book – that's how bad the language was.

When complaints to security were ignored and other spectators turned a blind eye, the abuse got worse. That's when my friend started filming – for evidence, not clout. If you're a woman, you'll get it. The lens didn't deter him, and he called her a stupid B, to which she asked, "Is that how you speak to all women?"

He replied, on camera, "No only c*nts like you," accompanied by his charming middle finger.

In shock, my friend tweeted out the video with the caption:

> Never have I or my sports loving girlfriends been so badly abused and sexually harassed. Went on for hours.

Perhaps not surprisingly, it was retweeted like an overcrowded aviary, and before we could finish our post-ordeal wine, the phone was ringing off the hook with media outlets asking for a comment.

I gave a couple of interviews that night but knew it would continue into the next day's news cycle. The fury that pulsed through my body made it impossible to sleep. When I received an early morning phone call, I was ready to unleash my voice.

"Just letting you know we had a burst water main in the city overnight, and it's a bit of a mess."

PART THREE

Oh, the unexpected call was from the control room of the water company I worked for. Less than an hour later, I was in the office fielding call after call after call.

"Are you calling about the burst or the boxing?" became my standard greeting. My voice switched from a riled up "it was racist, vulgar and sexually explicit" to a calm "crews are repairing the pipe and two lanes will remain closed while work is carried out."

I never thought I'd be pivoting from outbursts to actual bursts, but I'm so glad my voice skills allowed me to do that. Both stories served a positive community service, and they hit the sweet spot!

Perhaps the most unusual role I accessed with my voice came the year after my high school musical *Little Shop of Horrors*. They decided to drop the singing and dancing in favour of Shakespeare – right in my theatrical wheelhouse. I memorised monologues for fun on the weekend. Being an all-girls school, they had the brilliant idea to portray the greatest heterosexual love story of all time – *Romeo and Juliet*. It was actually a stroke of genius, as tickets sold like horny hotcakes with the entire population of the boys' school keen to see if two girls would kiss – under the guise of cultural enrichment.

Even though they needed two people to strap my chest down with bandages and stick fake hair on my face, my deep resonant voice got me the role of Romeo, oh Romeo. It was awesome. We were even taught how to sword fight by someone who worked on the lightsaber scenes in *Star Wars*. That was quite a cool door my voiceprint allowed me to open.

My clients open doors with their voiceprints every day.

- Katie went from feeling awkward on camera and trying to be someone she wasn't to owning her individuality and blowing up on Instagram. Last count was more than 150K followers!
- After initially being told her voice "wasn't good enough," Emma went on to record the audiobook version of her story in her own voice – as it should be!
- Public speaking once filled Melanie with dread. Now she's opened doors to the speaking mother lode – podcasts, panels, webinars, social media videos and keynotes on stage in front of hundreds.

PART THREE

- Susan used to feel like a small-town country woman. Today she's a confident communicator who has shared stages with high-profile names and even appeared on national television.

Speaking of television, I've also helped hundreds of young broadcast journalists find their voice, not just on air, but behind the scenes, opening doors in a competitive and often brutal media industry. There's rarely a day I turn on the news – any station – without seeing one of my students crushing it – reading the bulletin, presenting the weather or reporting live from major international events.

And for my multilingual clients, their voiceprint becomes an even more potent access code – allowing them to transmit their message across cultures and continents.

Take a moment to reflect: What doors has your voice already opened?

Because having a strong voiceprint means carrying a powerful passport. A high-level security clearance.

An access-all-areas swipe card to people, places and possibilities.

All you need to decide is, where will your voice take you next?

"Don't be so scared to make the 'wrong' mark with your voiceprint that you end up making no mark at all."

SALLY PROSSER

CHAPTER 16
PRINT IT ON THE RECORD

"Good morning, it's five thirty, I'm Sally Prosser with your news update. First to weather, and a sine and mostly funny day ahead."

That faux pas actually happened to me live on radio in one of my first jobs. *Sine* and mostly *funny*, instead of *fine* and mostly *sunny*. It was pretty funny, and by far not the worst mistake I made either. When I ran 7 Local News in Central Queensland, I once played the same story two nights in a row! (I chose not to report on the spike in cases of deja vu.) When I produced TV news for Network 10, I wrongly advised a reporter on the pronunciation of a well-known Gold Coast suburb. (Put the '*pimp*' not the '*palm*' in Pimpama for those playing at home.)

PART THREE

And back in those sine and mostly funny radio days, I accidentally told the good people of Wollongong the rubbish tip was *free* for the day. In my defence, I was in my early 20s, lived at home and had never renovated, so the value of the local dump was lost on me.

A flustered council worker rang the newsroom. "Love! Are you telling people the tip's free?" I started madly re-reading the press release. "We've got cars lined up all the way down the road, they're blocking the highway."

I felt the odd combination of both panicked and chuffed – *I didn't realise so many people listened to 96.5 Wave FM!* I then had to issue an awkward clarification that you could go to the tip and pick up *mulch* for free, not dump for free.

So why am I opening this chapter telling you about my royal f-ups?

Mistakes are your greatest teacher.

Since the dump drama, I've learnt a lot, beyond just reading things more carefully. One of the biggest insights that really helps me as a voice and public speaking coach is this: a major reason people avoid speaking up, unmuting themselves, or taking the mic is the fear of saying the 'wrong' thing. They're terrified of making a mistake, as if once they've spoken, their voice is printed on the record forever and can't be erased or edited.

Maybe this is you.

Maybe you're worried you'll mess up a word or not be able to answer a question, and then *they'll* think *you* don't know what you're talking about. And just like that, your credibility is crushed; your reputation is in ruins; you're fired; you're cancelled, and by sunset you're on the street eating cat food out of a tin. That kind of negative spiral thinking is what I call *cat*-astrophising. I know it well. Mine usually ends with – *you know it* – lying in the fetal position on the couch rocking my bottle of merlot.

That's what I was doing one evening watching myself talk shit on national TV. Literally. "Does it smell? Does it leave skid marks? And where does the poo go?"

There I was on the silver screen in my bright green company T-shirt, long blonde hair and a big smile to match the cheekiness of the topic. I was spokesperson for a major water and sewerage company, and we'd launched Australia's first poo-powered car. Now, before you get images of poop-scooping at the petrol pump, I'll clarify – it was an electric car, charged at a sewage treatment plant by energy generated from wastewater.

Little aside, too good not to share: we actually won a prestigious PR award for this campaign – and the man to present it? Shane Jacobson, better known as Kenny, the star of a mockumentary about a plumber! That's the definition of 'apt' right there.

The merlot moment on the couch was before these accolades, and I was having a crisis of confidence on the toilet humour. *Are they laughing* at *me? Laughing* with *me? Laughing* for *me?* My phone rang. It was the CEO. No need for a voice verification check on this one. It was clearly her.

"Hi Sally."

I held my breath and braced for impact.

"I *loved* the sound bite that got picked up by *The Project*!"

Phew! It *was* great coverage. What a relief the big boss felt the same.

The stakes are definitely higher when you're speaking on behalf of a whole organisation. Executives consistently rate 'reputation' as one of the top strategic risks their companies face.[6] Maybe your speaking scenarios carry this type of high-stakes risk?

Who are you speaking on behalf of?

This question can motivate, but it can also deter. One of the main reasons companies hire me for media training is to help their people feel more confident to put themselves forward for 'on-the-record' opportunities.

I used to think catastrophising was just something I did, because as a journalist and PR professional you're wired for worst-case scenario. Many a frantic phone call with Mum ended in her reminding me, "It's PR, not ER, honey." Turns out negative thought spirals are very common regardless of your career background.

Have you ever made a small mistake in a presentation, and it snowballed into a full-blown identity crash? Or you saw someone walk out while you were speaking and assumed it was because they hate you? Or you stumbled on one word, and it descended into a complete capitulation of the speech?

And the wild thing is, a lot of catastrophising happens before anything even goes 'wrong'.

- *What if I forget my speech?*
- *What if I say something silly?*

PART THREE

- *What if I can't answer a question?*
- *What if my voice breaks?*
- *What if I get it wrong and can't take it back?*

You become so afraid to make a 'wrong' mark with your voiceprint, you end up making no mark at all. And *that* is the biggest error.

In the public relations world, there's a great phrase: define or be defined. No comment *is* a comment, and staying quiet does not mean your story goes away; it means someone else writes it for you. Would you rather run the risk of making a smudge with your voiceprint or be completely silenced or falsely represented?

You name a public speaking stuff-up, and I've probably got a story about it. From slides reformatting in front of a national convention (voiceprint became viceprint) to wardrobe malfunctions in opening keynotes (I almost took an eye out with my mid-bust button snapping). There was that time I dramatically threw my hairbrush off stage as part of a lip-syncing extravaganza, only for it to hit my laptop and cut the music. The sky didn't fall in. I'm here to tell the tale. And I'm all the better for it.

In fact, when I profusely apologised to that council worker on the phone, he said, "Don't worry about it love, most people thought it was too good to be true." And the tip had its highest revenue Saturday in a long while!

Three ways to stop catastrophising

1. **Get specific**
   General exaggerations are the fuel for negative thinking spirals.

   "Oh, I'll make a mistake, and they'll hate me."

   - *What mistake specifically?*
   - *Who are 'they'?*
   - *How do you know they'll hate you?*
   - *Why do you care if they hate you?*

   I've spent many coaching sessions relentlessly drilling down on specifics to help people realise most problems are of their own creation.

2. **Flip *what if* for *if I***
   Replace "what if I forget my words?" with "if I forget my words I'll *(insert strategy)*."

   This shifts you from being reactive to

proactive. Your strategies could be things like:

- *Looking at your notes*
- *Taking a breath*
- *Throwing to another speaker*

There are countless strategies – and a coach can help you discover them.

3. **Use the 5-5-5 rule**

   Ask: "Will this matter in five minutes, five days or five years?"

   This really puts things in perspective – like the PR, not ER phrase!

> **Putting your voiceprint on the record is a risk worth taking.**

People will say nasty things. People will say nice things. People will say nice things to your face and nasty things behind your back. People will say mean things when you're alive and flattering things when you're dead.

Trying to please everyone is a zero-sum game. Nobody wins, and you're guaranteed to lose.

Mum, aka Queen of the Quote, always shared the saying: "You can be the best, juiciest peach in the box, and you have to accept that some people just don't like peaches."

Above all, don't be scared of getting it wrong, accept that you *will*. It's the only way to get things 'right'. Your voiceprint deserves to be out in the world. Not hidden. Not hesitated.

So *go on*, fearlessly print it on the record.

"We will never know the people who *almost* spoke up and changed lives."

SALLY PROSSER

CHAPTER 17
TAKE THE GLOVES OFF

I love a good heist movie. *Yes,* give me *The Italian Job, Ocean's Eleven* or *The Thomas Crown Affair* any rainy day. I'm eating cheese, sipping wine and backing the charming thief every time! Whether they're pinching a painting, cracking a safe or dealing with diamonds – they always wear gloves, and the hero never gets caught. No fingerprints, no DNA, no evidence left behind.

> **Speaking is not a robbery you want to get away with.**

In fact, your voice slipping away unnoticed is the real crime. It's robbing people who need to hear you and stealing the joy of expression from yourself. Taking off the gloves is a declaration that you're done sanitising yourself for the sake of others. You're not scared to be identified. You're proud to be seen and heard.

In the book *The Top Five Regrets of the Dying* by Bronnie Ware, the number three regret is people wishing they had the courage to express themselves.[7] They regret the things they didn't say, not the things they did. And let's be real: if you're lucky enough to get a deathbed to contemplate life on, you're *not* going to lie there thinking:

- *Oh, I shouldn't have posted that video, Jenny from my old primary school might judge me.*
- *Why did I tell my story on stage? My face went so red and blotchy.*
- *I never should've volunteered for that presentation – Simon from sales looked miffed.*
- *Damn making those TikToks! I should've listened to the commenter who said my unbrushed eyelashes looked like squished bugs.*

> **The reasons we keep our voiceprint gloves on in life look ridiculous in the face of death. We will *never know* the people who *almost* spoke up and changed lives.**

Don't be one of those people. Someone is waiting to hear *your* story in *your* voice.

> **Impact doesn't come from perfection; it comes from presence.**

And presence doesn't just happen – it's charged by confidence and strengthened by experience. You earn it every time you do something that feels hard. Every time you feel the fear and do it anyway. Every time you feel the shake and show up anyway.

Confidence is a muscle, and you build it by proving you can do things you didn't think you could do. Trust me, I know this firsthand.

I did *not* think I could survive a 10-day silent meditation course. Far out, I hardly made it through the first night of that first 36-hour silent retreat when we had the soup. You see, after dinner we went to the meditation hall for a pre-lights-out yoga nidra. As I

PART THREE

lay on my back drifting into the blissful state between waking and sleeping – my belly grumbled. *Oh dear.* Another grumble. *This isn't good.* The usual shit that came out of my mouth on a Friday night was finding another way.

That motion moved more than dinner. It birthed a new era of myself. It was the turning point for less drinking and more spiritual connection.

Getting out of your comfort zone does this.

> **Growth doesn't happen in comfort.**
> **Comfort doesn't lead to growth.**
> **You get to pick one.**

On the Snowy Mountains expedition, I didn't think I'd even make it to that icy river. The day before, I trekked up the treacherous Dead Horse Gap in practically my underwear. Ninety minutes of incline in snow shoes. The wind was biting; my breath was straining, and I could hardly see my next step. Sporting leopard-print activewear, I summoned my spirit animals, mouthed the lyrics of 'Unstoppable' by Sia and leaned on the group to get me there.

And I did it! I reached the summit. Negative 8 degrees Celsius in nothing but bike shorts, a crop top and my love-heart sunglasses. The moment was overwhelming, and my eyes welled. I had done something I didn't think *any* human could do, yet here *I* was doing it – and feeling amazing.

What else can I do that I think I can't? The tears flowed, washing away the old beliefs. They didn't poetically flow though; they froze midway down my face and blurred my vision – so I needed to stop being emotional for safety reasons. The tears *really* flowed in the hot shower later that night!

I'd come so far from being pinned to the bed at my rock bottom. From mattress to mountain top, where the gloves were literally and metaphorically off!

Yet this story may never have been told. If I'd never released a podcast or posted my first social media video or said *yes* when invited to speak at an event – you'd certainly not be reading this book right now.

A message without a voice is like an aspiring nail model wearing mittens.

PART THREE

What message will the world miss because you chose not to take off the gloves?

I implore you: be braver. Be bolder. Be fully expressed.

Three ways you can use your voice right now

1. Call instead of email.

2. Voice note instead of text.

3. Post a video or voiceover on socials instead of a graphic (and if you're stuck on content, read your favourite part of this book!)

"Take your mark."

I was 10 years old on the lane four block ready to dive in the pool for my pet event – the 50 m butterfly. The gun went off. Everyone dived into the water. Except me.

I froze – not because I doubted my stroke, but

because the water was too chilly. That old story of me hating the cold took hold. I stood up shivering, stepped off the block, scurried to my bag and zipped myself into a big, fluffy, furry coat.

My dad was furiously perplexed and shook his head. "Sal," he said, "what's the point of all your talent and all your training if you won't bloody dive in the pool?!"

That line hit harder than the cold ever could. And maybe it's the line you need to hear too.

You can have all the speaking talent and read all the books, but it won't change anything unless you dive in the pool. You need to step forward and courageously use your voice. Get your gorgeous, grubby, imperfectly perfect voiceprints all over every room you walk into.

Let people know you were there.
Let people hear who you are.

You're not here to slip away unnoticed.

This isn't a heist. Take the gloves off.

Leave an impression that lasts.

Imprint your voiceprint – bold, clear and undeniably yours.

VOICEPRINT MANIFESTO

I promise to use my voice.
My voice is not an afterthought –
it is my power, my presence, my legacy.

Some days, it might feel like I'm speaking
into the void.
Like no one's listening, and my
words are drowning in the noise.

Take a deep breath.

VOICEPRINT MANIFESTO

Listen to the voice of your Higher Self:
Remember who you are.
Remember everything you've overcome.
You survived your worst day.
Believe your best day is yet to come.

My voice is a powerful energetic channel.
A force. A frequency. A fingerprint.

I embrace the full force of my voice.
It carries my stories, my wisdom, my soul.

It vibrates with everything I have lived,
everything I have learnt,
and everything I am here to give.
It is magic. It is medicine. It is meant to be heard.

I will speak it. Declare it. Voice it.

VOICEPRINT MANIFESTO

I choose to speak with conviction.
I will not dilute my message to
make others comfortable.
I will not apologise for taking up space
or for standing firm in my truth.
I will not compare, shrink, or soften
my voice to fit expectations.

I know my voice leaves an imprint.
Every word I speak has the power to shape,
move, and inspire.
I will use my voice with purpose and courage.

I will not wait for permission.
I will not let fear, doubt, or judgement keep me quiet.
Impact doesn't come from perfection –
it comes from presence.

The time to speak is now.

The world needs my voice.

The gloves are off.
I show up; I speak up, and I make my mark.

ACKNOWLEDGEMENTS

Writing this book has been a deep practice in devotion, and I couldn't have done it alone.

To my speech and drama teacher Carole Miller – this book exists because of you. You were the first to nurture my voice, to teach me its power and to instil in me the love of expression that has shaped my life's work. I miss you.

Thank you also to the many other mentors, teachers and coaches who have guided me on my soul's path and helped me hone my craft.

To my supportive partner Patrick – thank you for always stopping what you were doing when I called down the stairs, "Baaaaabe, can I read you part of my book?" and telling me how great it was, even in the terrible early drafts. I am so grateful for your endless love and unwavering support.

To my dad – thank you for your love, lessons and vocal legacy. You always told me to do whatever floats my boat, and you'll be proud to know I am. I miss your voice.

To my mum – thank you for always having my back and supporting my dreams. For driving me to all those speech and drama lessons and supporting me at every eisteddfod, public speaking competition and high school production throughout the years. Thanks also for keeping me humble. "Just because Patrick thinks it's good, doesn't mean it's any good – he'd say you look good in a potato sack." LOL, yes, he would. You know how much I love you, Mum!

To my clients and Soul Speaker community – leading you to find, use and love your voice is a great privilege, and I am in awe of the work you put in and the courage you show.

To the team at Dean Publishing and Simon & Schuster – thank you for guiding me through the book publishing process and getting these pages in front of people.

And finally, to *you*, dear reader – thank you for believing in me enough to pick up this book. Pick up a microphone next and use your beautiful voice!

BONUSES

 Keen to learn more about how to leave a lasting impression every time you speak? I've put together my favourite resources – including special bonuses exclusively for readers of *Voiceprint* – at www.sallyprosser.online/voiceprint.

 And if you want to see my butt on the front page of the *Hobart Mercury* or me on top of that snowy mountain in the love-heart glasses and a whole bunch of photos that match the stories in the book, head to www.sallyprosser.com.au/book.

ABOUT THE AUTHOR

Sally Prosser is a sought-after voice and public speaking coach, speech writer and founder of Soul Speakers – a global community dedicated to helping people speak from the heart with confidence.

Sally opened a speech and drama school at just 16 and has been teaching speakers, leaders and creatives to embrace their voice ever since – whether on stage, on camera or in life.

With a background as a TV and radio news reporter, spokesperson for one of Australia's largest water companies and an award-winning entrepreneur, she

ABOUT THE AUTHOR

understands the power of voice in shaping influence and impact.

Sally holds a Licentiate Diploma in Speech & Drama Teaching and degrees in journalism and law from the University of Wollongong. As a master NLP, hypnosis, and reiki practitioner, Sal brings a unique blend of technical expertise and energetic alignment to her work. She believes your voice is more than just sound – it's the invisible mark you leave on the world.

When Sally's not coaching or speaking, she enjoys travelling the world with Patrick, practising yoga or doing jigsaw puzzles while bingeing a great show at their home in Brisbane, Australia.

Voiceprint is her first book.

Find Sally at www.sallyprosser.com.au, listen to *That Voice Podcast* and connect on social media @sallyprosservoice or LinkedIn, where she has 100+ recommendations.

Sally is available for speaking, workshops and private coaching.

PERMISSIONS

Special thanks to writer and creator Erica Mallett for permission to include her original concept of Cringe Mountain within this manuscript.

www.ericamallett.com

ENDNOTES

Part 1

1. Bloomberg (26 July 2024) '"I need to identify you": How one question saved Ferrari from a deepfake scam', *Bloomberg*, accessed 18 May 2025, https://www.bloomberg.com/news/articles/2024-07-26/ferrari-narrowly-dodges-deepfake-scam-simulating-deal-hungry-ceo.

2. Robins-Early N (20 May 2024) 'ChatGPT suspends Scarlett Johansson-like voice as actor speaks out against OpenAI', *The Guardian*, accessed 18 May 2025, https://www.theguardian.com/technology/article/2024/may/20/chatgpt-scarlett-johansson-voice.

3. Sensity (2024) 'The state of deepfakes', *Sensity*, accessed 18 May 2025, https://sensity.ai/reports/.

4. Tanaka YL and Kudo Y (2012) 'Effects of familiar voices on brain activity', *International Journal of Nursing Practice*, 2(38): 38–44. https://doi.org/10.1111/j.1440-172X.2012.02027.x.

5. DeStefano J (2023) 'Written statement of Jennifer DeStefano: Abuses of artificial intelligence', *United States Senate*, accessed 18 May 2025, https://www.judiciary.senate.gov/imo/media/doc/2023-06-13%20PM%20-%20Testimony%20-%20DeStefano.pdf.

6. Karimi F (2023) '"Mom, these bad men have me": She believes scammers cloned her daughter's voice in a fake kidnapping', *CNN*, accessed 18 May 2025, https://edition.cnn.com/2023/04/29/us/ai-scam-calls-kidnapping-cec/index.html.

7. Jogia J, Thomas J, Barbato M, and Bentall R (2024) 'Social anxiety, voice confrontation and voice recognition: A bilingual exploration', *International Journal of Psychology*, 59(6):1084–1090,

doi.org/10.1002/ijop.13234.

8   Mallett E (26 March 2023) 'Cringe Mountain™ Will Be My Legacy' [TikTok video], accessed 28 July 2025, https://www.tiktok.com/@erica_mallett/video/7214804177522871570?lang=en.

9   Chartrand TL and Bargh JA (1999) 'The chameleon effect: The perception–behavior link and social interaction', *Journal of Personality and Social Psychology*, 76(6): 893–910, https://doi.org/10.1037/0022-3514.76.6.893.

10 Jamieson JP, Nock MK and Mendes WB (2012) 'Mind over matter: Reappraising arousal improves cardiovascular and cognitive responses to stress', *Journal of Experimental Psychology: General*, 141(3): 417–422, https://doi.org/10.1037/a0025719.

11 Zaccaro A, Piarulli A, Laurino M, Garbella E, Menicucci D, Neri B and Gemignani A (2018) 'How breath-control can change your life: A systematic review on psycho-physiological correlates of slow breathing', *Frontiers in Human Neuroscience*, 12, https://doi.org/10.3389/fnhum.2018.00353.

12 Lung Foundation Australia (2025) 'How your lungs work', *Lung Foundation Australia*, accessed 18 May 2025, https://lungfoundation.com.au/lung-health/protecting-your-lungs/how-your-lungs-work/#:~:text=Every%20day%20we%20breathe%20about,all%2C%20a%20symbol%20of%20life.

13 Billiet L (director) (2020) *Freeman* [motion picture], General Strike and Matchbox Production, Australia.

Part 2

1   Vickhoff B, Malmgren H, Aström R, Nyberg G, Ekström S-R, Engwall M, Snygg J, Nilsson M and Jörnsten R (2013) 'Music structure determines heart rate variability of singers', *Frontiers in Psychology*, 4, https://doi.org/10.3389/fpsyg.2013.00334.

2   Acosta A (2020) 'The philosophy of Om', *Journal of Iyengar Yoga London*, 52, https://iyengaryogalondon.co.uk/

the-science-and-philosophy-of-om-aum/.

3   Benson H, Beary JF and Carol MP (1974) 'The relaxation response', *Psychiatry,* 37(1): 37–46, https://doi.oirg/10.1080/0033 2747.1974.11023785.

4   Maniscalco M (2006) 'Humming, nitric oxide and paranasal sinus ventilation' [PhD thesis], *Karolinska Institutet,* accessed 18 May 2025, https://hdl.handle.net/10616/38896.

5   Chozick A (2023) 'Elizabeth Holmes Opens Up About Her Theranos trial and what comes next', *New York Times,* accessed 18 May 2025, https://www.nytimes.com/2023/05/07/business/elizabeth-holmes-theranos-interview.html.

6   University of Berkeley (2015) 'Robin T. Lakoff: "What's up with Upspeak?', *University of Berkeley,* accessed 18 May 2025, https://matrix.berkeley.edu/research-article/whats-upspeak/.

7   Hills A (2 January 2008) 'Adam Hills - Australian accents', *Chocchipfox*, YouTube, accessed 28 July 2025, https://youtu.be/KpBYnL5fAXE.

8   Jensen MP, Adachi T, and Hakimian S (2015) 'Brain Oscillations, Hypnosis, and Hypnotizability', *The American Journal of Clinical Hypnosis*, 57(3): 230–253, doi.org/10.1080/00029157.2014.976786.

9   Eleftheriou-Smith L-M (2017) 'Dutch teenager Vera Mol died bungee jumping due to Spanish instructor's "poor English"', *Independent,* accessed 18 May 2025, https://www.independent.co.uk/news/world/europe/vera-mol-bungee-jump-death-spanish-instructor-poor-english-no-jump-dutch-teenager-a7809726.html.

10 Mount H (2013) 'The secret to a great tongue twister', *News.com.au*, accessed 18 May 2025, https://www.news.com.au/lifestyle/health/mental-health/the-secret-to-a-great-tongue-twister/news-story/3bc0a68f33b66c3f937dbcff0f37d922.

11 Guinness World Records (2020) 'The sixth sick sheik's sixth sheep's sick'[X status], accessed 18 May 2025, https://x.com/GWR/status/1244920812970393600?s=20.

12. Miller N, Maruyama G, Beaber RJ, and Valone K (1976) 'Speed of speech and persuasion', *Journal of Personality and Social Psychology*, 34(4):615–624, doi.org/10.1037/0022-3514.34.4.615.

13. Cabane OF (2013) *The Charisma Myth: How Anyone Can Master the Art and Science of Personal Magnetism*, Portfolio.

Part 3

1. Aucouturier J, Johansson P, Hall L, Segnini R, Mercadié L, and Watanabe K (2016) 'Covert digital manipulation of vocal emotion alter speakers' emotional states in a congruent direction', *Proceedings of the National Academy of Sciences of the United States of America*, 113(4):948–953, doi.org/10.1073/pnas.1506552113..

2. Grosso F, Barbiani D, Cavalera C, Volpato E, and Pagnini F (2024) 'Risk Factors Associated with Nocebo Effects: A Review of Reviews,' *Brain, Behavior, and Immunity*, 38, doi.org/10.1016/j.bbih.2024.100800.

3. Radin D, Hayssen G, Emoto M, and Kizu T (2006) 'Double-Blind Test of the Effects of Distant Intention on Water Crystal Formation', *Explore*, 2(5): 408–411, doi.org/10.1016/j.explore.2006.06.004.

4. Van der Kolk B (2014) *The Body Keeps the Score: Brain, Mind, and Body in the Healing of Trauma*, Penguin Books.

5. Delimon K (2023) *Trust the Flames: My Wild Ride from Mindlessness to Mindfulness*, Katie Delimon.

6. Deloitte (2013) 'Exploring strategic risk: 300 executives around the world say their view of strategic risk is changing', *Deloitte*, accessed 18 May 2025, https://djcs-prod.s3.amazonaws.com/public/blogs/deloitte/blogs.dir/7/files/2013/10/strategic_risk_survey.pdf.

7. Ware B (2012) *The top five regrets of the dying: A life transformed by the dearly departing*, Hay House.

AUDIOBOOK

Voiceprint is also available in audio format.

Jump onto your favourite audiobook platform to have the story narrated for you by the author.

ORACLE CARDS

This deck is for soul-led creators who long to express their truth with clarity and confidence.

Whether you are stepping on stage, recording your message or simply finding the courage to speak from the heart, these cards will help you discover the hidden codes within your voice.

Scan the QR code to purchase

www.ingramcontent.com/pod-product-compliance
Lightning Source LLC
Chambersburg PA
CBHW031241290426
44109CB00012B/381